Social Studies

myWorld
ACTIVITY GUIDE
4

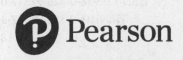

Pearson

Boston, Massachusetts   **Chandler, Arizona**
Glenview, Illinois   **New York, New York**

This work is solely for the use of instructors and administrators for the purpose of teaching courses and assessing student learning. Unauthorized dissemination, publication or sale of the work, in whole or in part (including posting on the Internet) will destroy the integrity of the work and is strictly prohibited.

Credits appear on page 214, which constitutes an extension of this copyright page.

ISBN-13: 978-0-328-97317-0
ISBN-10: 0-328-97317-3
3 18

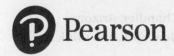

Contents

Chapter 4

Chapter 5

Chapter 6

Chapter 7

Chapter 8

Chapter 9

Graphic Organizers

myWorld Activity Guide

How to Use This Book

The *myWorld Activity Guide* was designed for teachers who love social studies but want to teach it in a different way. The program focuses on key topics in social studies, aligning to content frequently taught in each grade from kindergarten to Grade 5. The chapters in this book introduce students to social studies through fun activities and engaging inquiries. You can use the Activity Guide on its own, with associated support materials, or in connection with your basal program.

Teacher Planner

The Chapter Planner outlines the chapter's content in a clear chart with this information:

- **Description** gives a quick overview of each activity and its steps

- **Duration** offers a time estimate, making it easy to plan

- **Materials** lists the materials you will need for each part of the lesson

- **Participants** suggests whether to complete each part of the activity as whole class, small group, or individual

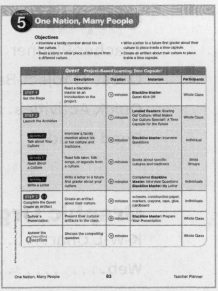

Quest

Each chapter includes detailed lesson suggestions for a long-term inquiry, or Quest.

- Each Quest starts with a Compelling Question, designed to engage students in the inquiry.

- The Quest is set up with three steps: Set the Stage, Launch the Activities, and Complete the Quest.

- Within each step, you'll find suggestions for guiding students to complete a series of activities, culminating in a final product, such as a hands-on project, presentation, civic discussion, or writing project.

- Each chapter contains suggestions for modifying the activities for English Learners.

- Where appropriate, student worksheets are provided to support student completion of the Quest.

- Rubrics in the front of the book will help you and your students evaluate their work.

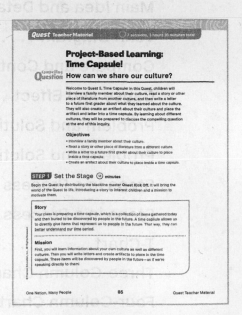

Quick Activities

Each chapter includes detailed lesson suggestions for a series of short activities related to the chapter content. Where appropriate, student worksheets are provided to support student completion of activities. Rubrics in the front of this book will help you and your students evaluate their work on each activity. The Activity Guide also offers suggestions for modifying the activities for English Learners.

Examples of Quick Activities are:

Games	Preparing and Acting Out a Skit
Debates	Building a Social Media Profile
Art Projects	Map Activities

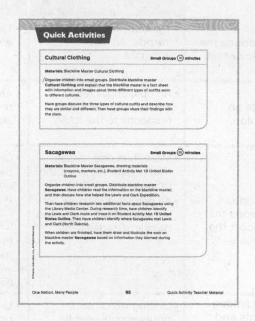

Read Aloud or Readers Theater

Each chapter has a Read Aloud or Readers Theater related to chapter content. With grade-appropriate language, the stories and Readers Theaters bring to life important content related to the chapter.

Graphic Organizers

You will find a wide variety of graphic organizers at the back of this book. You will find many uses for them as your students complete the activities and Quests described in this book.

How to Use This Book

Opinion Writing

Directions: Copy the rubric for individuals or groups (for collaborative writing projects). Rank individuals or groups for each skill.

	4 Excellent	3 Good	2 Satisfactory	1 Needs Improvement
Introduce the topic or text.	• The topic is clearly introduced and is accurate.	• The topic is introduced and is mostly accurate.	• An attempt is made to introduce the topic, but it is incorrect and/or unclear.	• The topic is not introduced.
State an opinion.	• An opinion is clearly stated and accurately responds to the topic.	• An opinion that mostly responds to the topic is stated but is vague.	• An attempt is made to state an opinion, but it does not respond to the topic and/or is unclear.	• An opinion is not stated.
Provide reasons that support the opinion.	• More than one reason that clearly supports the opinion is provided. • All provided reasons are supported with facts and details. (Grades 4–5)	• Only one reason is provided or more than one reason is provided, but the reasons mostly support the opinion. (Grade 3) • Provided reasons are mostly supported with facts and details. (Grades 4–5)	• An attempt is made to provide a reason, but the reason is either unclear or does not support the opinion. (Grade 3) • Facts and details do not clearly support the provided reasons. (Grades 4–5)	• No reasons are provided. (Grade 3) • Provided reasons are not supported with facts or details. (Grades 4–5)
Use linking words and phrases to connect opinion and reasons.	• Linking words and phrases consistently are used correctly to connect the opinion and reasons.	• Linking words and phrases are generally used correctly to connect the opinion and reasons.	• Linking words and phrases are used incorrectly to connect the opinion and reasons.	• Linking words and phrases are not used to connect the opinion and reasons.
Provide a concluding statement or section.	• A concluding statement or section is provided and includes a clear restatement of the opinion without introducing new ideas. (Grade 3) • A concluding statement or section is provided that clearly relates to the opinion without introducing new ideas. (Grades 4–5)	• A concluding statement or section is provided, but it includes a vague restatement of the opinion or introduces new ideas. (Grade 3) • A concluding statement or section is provided that generally relates to the opinion or introduces new ideas. (Grades 4–5)	• An attempt is made to provide a concluding statement or section, but it includes a vague restatement of the opinion and new ideas. (Grade 3) • A concluding statement or section is provided that vaguely relates to the opinion and introduces new ideas. (Grades 4–5)	• A concluding statement or section is not provided.

Informative/Explanatory Writing

Directions: Copy the rubric for individuals or groups (for collaborative writing projects). Rank individuals or groups for each skill.

	4 Excellent	3 Good	2 Satisfactory	1 Needs Improvement
Introduce a topic.	• The topic is clearly introduced and is accurate.	• The topic is introduced and is mostly accurate.	• An attempt is made to introduce the topic but is incorrect and/or unclear.	• The topic is not introduced.
Group related information together.	• Related information is clearly and consistently grouped together.	• Related information is mostly grouped together.	• Related information is sometimes grouped together, but organization of other information is unclear.	• Related information is not grouped together.
Develop the topic with facts, definitions, and details.	• Consistently provides facts, definitions, and details to develop the topic.	• Generally provides facts, definitions, and details to develop the topic.	• Gives some facts, definitions, and details, but they are inaccurate or have a vague link to the topic.	• No information, facts, or definitions are provided.
Use linking words and phrases to connect ideas within categories of information.	• Linking words and phrases consistently are used correctly to connect ideas within categories of information.	• Linking words and phrases are generally used correctly to connect ideas within categories of information.	• Linking words and phrases are used incorrectly to connect ideas within categories of information.	• Linking words and phrases are not used to connect ideas within categories of information.
Provide a concluding statement or section.	• A concluding statement or section is provided and includes a clear restatement of the topic without introducing new ideas. (Grade 3) • A concluding statement or section is provided that clearly relates to the information or explanation presented without introducing new ideas. (Grades 4–5)	• A concluding statement or section is provided, but it includes a vague restatement of the topic or introduces new ideas. (Grade 3) • A concluding statement or section is provided that generally relates to the information or explanation presented or introduces new ideas. (Grades 4–5)	• An attempt is made to provide a concluding statement or section, but it includes a vague restatement of the topic and new ideas. (Grade 3) • A concluding statement or section is provided that vaguely relates to the information or explanation presented and introduces new ideas. (Grades 4–5)	• A concluding statement or section is not provided.

Narrative Writing

Directions: Copy the rubric for individuals or groups (for collaborative writing projects). Rank individuals or groups for each skill.

	4 Excellent	3 Good	2 Satisfactory	1 Needs Improvement
Establish a situation and introduce a narrator and/or characters.	• The situation and the narrator and/or characters are clearly established.	• The situation and the narrator and/or characters are somewhat established.	• The situation and the narrator and/or characters are established but are vague.	• The situation and the narrator and/or characters are not established.
Organize an event sequence that unfolds naturally.	• The event sequence is organized so that it unfolds naturally.	• The event sequence is mostly organized so that it unfolds naturally.	• The event sequence is somewhat organized, but the events unfold awkwardly.	• The event sequence is not organized.
Use dialogue and descriptions to develop experiences and events.	• Dialogue and descriptions are used to clearly and effectively develop experiences and events.	• Some dialogue and descriptions are used to develop experiences and events.	• Dialogue and descriptions are used to develop experiences and events but are vague.	• No dialogue and descriptions are used to develop experiences and events.
Use temporal words and phrases to signal event order. (Grade 3)	• Temporal words and phrases are used consistently and accurately to signal event order.	• Temporal words and phrases are sometimes used to accurately signal event order.	• Temporal words and phrases are occasionally used to signal event order and/or are used inaccurately.	• Temporal words and phrases are not used.
Use a variety of transitional words and phrases to manage the sequence of events. (Grades 4–5)	• A variety of transitional words and phrases are used consistently and accurately to manage the sequence of events.	• A variety of transitional words and phrases are sometimes used to accurately manage the sequence of events.	• Transitional words and phrases are occasionally used to manage the sequence of events and may be used inaccurately or repetitively.	• Transitional words and phrases are not used to manage the sequence of events.
Use concrete words and phrases and sensory details to convey experiences and events. (Grades 4–5)	• Concrete words and phrases and sensory details are used consistently and accurately to convey experiences and events.	• Concrete words and phrases and sensory details are sometimes used to accurately convey experiences and events.	• Concrete words and phrases and sensory details are occasionally used to convey experiences and events and may be used inaccurately or repetitively.	• Concrete words and phrases and sensory details are not used to convey experiences and events.
Provide a sense of closure. (Grade 3)	• A strong sense of closure is provided with a clear ending.	• A sense of closure is provided with a vague ending.	• An attempt is made to provide closure with an ending that trails off.	• A sense of closure is not provided.
Provide a conclusion that follows from the narrated experiences or events. (Grades 4–5)	• A conclusion that clearly follows from the narrated experiences or events is provided.	• A conclusion that mostly follows from the narrated experiences or events is provided.	• A conclusion that loosely follows from the narrated experiences or events is provided.	• A conclusion that follows from the narrated experiences or events is not provided.

Project-Based Learning

Directions: Copy the rubric for individuals or groups. Rank individuals or groups for each skill as they conduct research to complete an inquiry project.

	4 Excellent	3 Good	2 Satisfactory	1 Needs Improvement
PLAN THE INQUIRY: Collaborate to develop a project plan.	• Assigns and accepts tasks within the group, encouraging all group members to play a role and contribute equally. • Engages effectively in collaborative discussions about the inquiry for the duration of the project by explicitly building on others' ideas and expressing their own clearly. • Participates fully in identifying details of the final outcome.	• Accepts tasks within the group, generally encouraging group members to play a role and contribute equally. • Engages in collaborative discussions about the inquiry by building on others' ideas and expressing their own. • Participates in identifying the details for the final outcome.	• Sometimes accepts tasks within the group, occasionally encouraging group members to play a role and contribute equally. • Sometimes engages in collaborative discussions about the inquiry by attempting to build on others' ideas and mostly expressing their own. • Participates somewhat in identifying the details for the final outcome.	• Rarely accepts tasks within the group or encourages group members to play a role and contribute equally. • Rarely engages in collaborative discussions about the inquiry, does not build on others' ideas, and rarely expresses their own. • Does not participate in identifying the details for the final outcome.
DO YOUR RESEARCH: Find sources to support your inquiry.	• Finds relevant evidence in support of own interpretations. • Routinely asks and answers questions, referring to the text to clarify meaning. • Reads or explores a number of sources to gain, modify, or extend knowledge or to learn different perspectives. • Always synthesizes and draws conclusions from information acquired through research.	• Generally finds relevant evidence in support of own interpretations. • Usually asks and answers questions, referring to the text to clarify meaning. • Reads or explores at least one source to gain, modify, or extend knowledge or to learn different perspectives. • Generally synthesizes and draws conclusions from information acquired through research.	• Finds some evidence in support of own interpretations, but some may be irrelevant. • Occasionally asks and answers questions, referring to the text to clarify meaning. • Attempts to read or explore sources but struggles to gain, modify, or extend knowledge. • Attempts to synthesize and draw conclusions from information acquired through research, but conclusions are vague or inaccurate.	• Finds little or no evidence in support of own interpretations. • Rarely or never asks and answers questions or refers to the text to clarify meaning. • Does not attempt to read or explore sources to gain, modify, or extend knowledge. • Does not synthesize or draw conclusions from information acquired through research.
PRODUCE THE PRODUCT: Demonstrate understanding of key ideas.	• Expresses and refines understanding of new concepts while creating the product. • Consistently uses language acquired from research in speaking and writing about the product. • Adds multiple visuals or multimedia components to enhance the product.	• Generally expresses and refines understanding of new concepts while creating the product. • Generally uses language acquired from research in speaking and writing about the product. • Adds at least one visual or multimedia to enhance the product.	• Occasionally expresses and refines understanding of new concepts while creating the product. • Occasionally uses language acquired from research in speaking and writing about the product. • Adds a visual or multimedia, but it is irrelevant and does not enhance the product.	• Rarely expresses and refines understanding of new concepts while creating the product. • Rarely uses language acquired from research in speaking and writing about the product. • Does not include a visual or multimedia.
REFLECT ON THE INQUIRY: Discuss the Compelling Question.	• Fully articulates a meaningful response to the Compelling Question.	• Generally articulates a meaningful response to the Compelling Question.	• Attempts to articulate a response to the Compelling Question, but the response is vague or irrelevant.	• Does not attempt to respond to the Compelling Question.

Collaborative Discussion

Directions: Copy the rubric for individuals, pairs, or groups as they engage in collaborative discussions with diverse partners about grade-appropriate topics and texts, including discussions about current local, national, and international issues. Rank individuals or groups for each skill.

	4 Excellent	3 Good	2 Satisfactory	1 Needs Improvement
Come to discussions prepared.	• Reads/studies all discussion materials prior to discussion. • Explicitly uses information and advance preparation to explore ideas during discussion.	• Reads/studies most discussion materials prior to discussion. • Mostly uses information and advance preparation to explore ideas during discussion.	• Reads/studies some discussion materials prior to discussion. • Occasionally uses information and advanced preparation to explore ideas during discussion.	• Reads/studies little if any discussion materials prior to discussion. • Does not use information and advanced preparation to explore ideas during discussion.
Follow agreed-upon rules for discussions.	• Follows agreed-upon rules at all times. • Carries out all assigned roles. (G4–5) • Consistently uses deliberative processes when making group decisions.	• Follows agreed-upon rules most of the time. • Carries out most assigned roles. (G4–5) • Generally uses deliberative processes when making group decisions.	• Follows agreed-upon rules but needs occasional direction. • Carries out some assigned roles with direction and reminders. (G4–5) • Sometimes uses deliberative processes when making group decisions.	• Does not follow agreed-upon rules without teacher direction. • Does not carry out assigned roles. (G4–5) • Does not use deliberative processes when making group decisions.
Pose and respond to specific questions to clarify or follow up on information.	• Uses questions and responses that explicitly clarify or follow up on the information presented and purposefully contributes to the discussion. • Poses questions that clearly link to the remarks of others.	• Uses questions and responses that generally clarify or follow up on the information presented and contributes to the discussion. • Poses questions that mostly link to the remarks of others.	• Attempts to use questions and responses that clarify or follow up on the information presented and attempts to contribute to the discussion. • Poses questions that vaguely link to the remarks of others.	• Does not use questions or responses that clarify or follow up on the information presented and does not contribute to the discussion. • Does not pose questions that link to the remarks of others.
Report on a topic.	• Thoroughly explains ideas and understanding in light of the discussion. • Expresses key ideas clearly. (G4–5) • Always provides facts that are appropriate to the discussion and details that are descriptive and relevant. • Always speaks clearly at an understandable pace. • Consistently raises reasons and evidence supporting particular points. (G4–5)	• Mostly explains ideas and understanding in light of the discussion. • Generally expresses key ideas clearly. (G4–5) • Usually provides facts that are appropriate to the discussion and details that are descriptive and relevant. • Generally speaks clearly at an understandable pace. • Mostly raises reasons and evidence supporting particular points. (G4–5)	• Attempts to explain ideas and understanding in light of the discussion. • Occasionally expresses key ideas, but they may not be clear. (G4–5) • Provides facts and details, but some facts and details may not be descriptive or relevant. • Attempts to speak clearly at an understandable pace but is difficult to understand at times. • Occasionally raises reasons and evidence, but these do not always support particular points. (G4–5)	• Rarely explains ideas and understanding in light of the discussion. • Rarely if ever expresses key ideas. (G4–5) • Does not provide facts or details. • Does not speak clearly or at an understandable pace. • Rarely if ever raises reasons and evidence supporting particular points. (G4–5)

Readers Theater/Read Aloud

Directions: Copy the rubric for individuals or groups. Rank individuals or groups for each skill.

	4 Excellent	3 Good	2 Satisfactory	1 Needs Improvement
BEFORE READING: Research and practice part.	• Plans own part and practices reading aloud with correct projection and diction. • Consistently uses context to confirm or self-correct word recognition and understanding, rereading as necessary. • Consistently applies grade-level phonics and word analysis skills in decoding words.	• Plans part with some assistance and practices reading aloud with mostly correct projection and diction. • Usually uses context to confirm or self-correct word recognition and understanding. • Usually applies grade-level phonics and word analysis skills in decoding words.	• Attempts to plan own part and practices reading aloud with sometimes incorrect projection and diction. • Occasionally uses context to confirm or self-correct word recognition and understanding. • Sometimes applies grade-level phonics and word analysis skills in decoding words.	• Does not plan own part or practice reading aloud. • Rarely if ever uses context to confirm or self-correct word recognition or understanding. • Rarely if ever applies grade-level phonics and word analysis skills in decoding words.
WHILE READING ALOUD OR PERFORMING: Communicate meaning with clear use of language and enthusiastic delivery.	• Consistently reads text with clear purpose and understanding, speaking clearly at an understandable pace. • Consistently reads prose orally with accuracy, appropriate rate, and expression on successive readings to support comprehension. • Understands the movement in front of a group; consistently maintains appropriate eye contact.	• Generally reads text with clear purpose and understanding, usually speaking clearly at an understandable pace. • Generally reads prose orally with accuracy, appropriate rate, and expression on successive readings to support comprehension. • Usually understands the movement in front of a group; usually maintains appropriate eye contact.	• Attempts to read text with purpose and understanding but sometimes does not speak clearly or at an understandable pace. • Reads prose orally but there are a few errors in accuracy, rate, and/or expression, even on successive readings. • Sometimes understands the movement in front of a group; attempts to maintain appropriate eye contact.	• Does not read text with clear purpose or understanding. • Does not read prose orally with accuracy, appropriate rate, or expression, even on successive readings. • Does not understand the movement in front of a group or maintain eye contact.
AFTER READING: Ask and answer questions about a reading of a text.	• Consistently asks clear questions related to the topic to check their own understanding of information presented. • Always links comments to the remarks of others. • Consistently offers appropriate elaboration and details.	• Often asks questions related to the topic to check their own understanding of information presented. • Often links comments to the remarks of others. • Often offers appropriate elaboration and details.	• Occasionally asks questions related to the topic to check their own understanding of information presented. • Occasionally links comments to the remarks of others. • Occasionally offers elaboration and details but may not be appropriate to the topic.	• Rarely if ever asks questions related to the topic to check their own understanding of information presented. • Rarely if ever links comments to the remarks of others. • Rarely if ever offers elaboration and details.
AFTER READING: Demonstrate comprehension of text.	• Accurately determines the main ideas and supporting details of a text read aloud. • Clearly distinguishes between own point of view and that of the narrator or characters.	• Usually determines the main ideas and supporting details of a text read aloud accurately. • Generally distinguishes between own point of view and that of the narrator or characters.	• Sometimes determines the main ideas and supporting details of a text read aloud but is not always accurate. • Has difficulty with distinguishing between own point of view and that of the narrator or characters.	• Rarely if ever determines the main ideas and supporting details of a text read aloud. • Is unable to distinguish between own point of view and that of the narrator or characters.

1 Geography of the United States

Objectives

- Identify geographical features such as mountains, plains, and bodies of water on a map.
- Recognize that bodies of water often form boundaries between states or countries.
- Create a map and label geographical features, bodies of water, natural resources, and climate details.

- Understand and use an inset map.
- Explain the water cycle.
- Identify and describe the five geographical regions of the United States.

Quest Project-Based Learning: Become a Cartographer

	Description	Duration	Materials	Participants
STEP 1 Set the Stage	Read a blackline master and an introduction to the project.	15 minutes	**Blackline Master:** Quest Kick Off	Whole Class
STEP 2 Launch the Activities	Discuss upcoming activities and background information.	5 minutes		Whole Class
Activity 1 ELL Tracking Lewis and Clark	Trace Lewis and Clark's route from St. Louis to the Pacific Ocean.	30 minutes	**Primary Source:** Tracking Lewis and Clark, Student Activity Mat 1A United States, atlas or other maps	Whole Class, Small Groups, Individual
Activity 2 History Detectives	Use clues in a journal entry to determine where William Clark was when he wrote it.	30 minutes	**Primary Source:** History Detectives, print atlases of the Oregon/Washington area, online maps	Whole Class, Individual
Activity 3 Water Boundaries	Examine a map to determine the location of bodies of water.	30 minutes	**Blackline Master:** Water Boundaries, other maps	Partners
Activity 4 Gather Map Sources	Study physical maps to understand how they represent geographical features.	30 minutes	Student Activity Mat 1A United States, online maps, print maps from the Library Media Center	Individual, Small Groups
Activity 5 Around the Nation	Play a game to demonstrate map reading skills.	30 minutes	**Blackline Master:** Around the Nation	Whole Class
STEP 3 Complete the Quest Make a Map	Create a map of a newly discovered island.	60 minutes	**Blackline Master:** Make a Map, poster board or art paper, drawing and coloring supplies	Individual
Answer the **Compelling Question**	Discuss the compelling question.	15 minutes		Whole Class

Quick Activities

	Description	Duration	Materials	Participants
Landforms Matching	Match landforms to their definitions in a class game.	20 minutes	Index cards, dictionaries, online geography resources	Partners, Whole Class
Water Cycle Collage	Assemble a water cycle collage.	30 minutes	**Blackline Master:** Water Cycle Collage, glue, scissors, construction paper	Individual
Climatologist in Training	Make educated guesses about the climate of an area.	15 minutes	**Leveled Readers:** *Our Weather; Weather; How Weather Works,* paper, pencil, online resources	Individual
Resources Word Search	Find resources in a puzzle and categorize them by type of resource.	10 minutes	**Blackline Master:** Resources Word Search, crayons, highlighters, or colored pencils	Individual, Whole Class
Update a Song ELL	Rewrite the lyrics to "This Land Is Your Land."	20 minutes	**Primary Source:** Update a Song, online geography resources, encyclopedias from the Library Media Center	Individual
Readers Theater: Big Moves	Read a conversation between friends who are comparing moves from one area to another.	20 minutes	**Readers Theater:** Big Moves	Small Groups

Project-Based Learning: Become a Cartographer

Compelling Question

How do the geographical features of a place make it unique?

Welcome to Quest 1, Become a Cartographer. In this Quest, students will study features of maps. They will use what they learn to construct their own original map of an imaginary place, which will prepare them to discuss the compelling question at the end of this inquiry.

Objectives

- Identify geographical features such as mountains, plains, and bodies of water on a map.
- Recognize that bodies of water often form boundaries between states or countries.
- Create a map and label geographical features, bodies of water, natural resources, and climate details.
- Understand and use an inset map.

STEP 1 Set the Stage ⑮ minutes

Begin the Quest by distributing the blackline master **Quest Kick Off.** It will bring the world of the Quest to life, introducing a story to interest students and a mission to motivate them.

Story

Tell students that once in a great while, new landmasses are created. Explain that a recent example of this is Shelly Island off the coast of Cape Hatteras, North Carolina, which suddenly appeared in early 2017 as a small strip of sand and has grown into a new beach since. Ask students to pretend something similar has happened in the middle of the Pacific Ocean. Because the landmass lies almost equidistant between the United States, Russia, and Japan, an international team of scientists from the three nations has been exploring the new island together. They have agreed to split the new island into three equal pieces, but they need an accurate map to do so.

Mission

Students must read a journal entry provided by the explorers to create a map (to scale) of the area, and also identify its position on the globe in an inset map. They must represent not only the geographical area but also physical features, climate, natural resources, and political boundaries.

STEP 2 Launch the Activities

The following five activities will help students prepare for their map project by helping them learn more about standard features of maps. Note that all five activities can be done independently of the larger Quest.

Activity 1   Tracking Lewis and Clark   (30) minutes

Materials: Primary Source: Tracking Lewis and Clark, Student Activity Mat 1A United States, atlas or other maps

Distribute the **Primary Source: Tracking Lewis and Clark,** which includes a journal entry from William Clark describing his proposed route from St. Louis to the Pacific Ocean. Also distribute Student Activity Mat 1A United States.

Before reading the journal entry as a class, explain to students that the journal entry is a primary source. This means it has been copied exactly as it was written, including spelling, capitalization, and punctuation. Then read the journal entry aloud to students as they follow along. This should help minimize the decrease in comprehension which the primary source might cause.

Ask students to look at their Student Activity Mat 1A United States as you read part of the first sentence. Have volunteers point out details in the sentence excerpt which seem important to mapping the Lewis and Clark trail. Then ask students to mark their maps based on the information in that sentence excerpt. Pause while they do so, before reading the next part of the sentence and repeating the process.

For your reference, Lewis and Clark refer to the present-day Clearwater River as "Kooskooske" in the passage.

When you reach the end of the first sentence, have students form groups of four and compare maps. Working together, have them reach a consensus on the trail location and correct their individual maps accordingly.

Next, talk through the second sentence with students to help them locate and mark a possible site for a trading post.

The location Clark describes is likely near the present-day cities of Vancouver, Washington, and Portland, Oregon, where the Columbia River and the Willamette River (known to them as the Multnomah River) converge. Use an atlas or other maps to locate this area if needed.

For an extra connection to Language Arts, consider having students work in groups to identify and correct the spelling, grammar, and punctuation of the journal entry.

Support for English Language Learners

Reading Provide each student with the Primary Source: Tracking Lewis and Clark.

Entering: Highlight key words for students on their copy of the journal entry (St. Louis, Missouri [River], Rocky Mountains, Columbia [River], and Pacific). Help them mark these locations on their maps and connect them with a line.

Emerging: Highlight key words for students on their copy of the journal entry (St. Louis, Missouri [River], Rocky Mountains, Columbia [River], and Pacific). Tell them to mark these locations on their maps and connect them with a line.

Developing: Ask students to read the first sentence and highlight the most important words they should use when tracing Lewis and Clark's path. Check their answers, correcting and adding as needed. Tell them to mark these locations on their maps and connect them with a line.

Expanding: Ask students to read the first sentence to themselves and then retell it in their own words. Check for accuracy and completeness before asking them to mark their maps.

Bridging: Ask students to read the passage to themselves and trace the Lewis and Clark trail on their maps independently. After, ask them what parts of the journal entry were unclear and have them suggest ways the writer could have made his message clearer to readers.

Activity 2 **History Detectives** **minutes**

Materials: Primary Source: History Detectives, print atlases of the Oregon/Washington area, online maps

Distribute the **Primary Source: History Detectives,** which includes a new journal entry from William Clark. Remind students that Lewis and Clark were on a mission to travel to the Pacific Ocean. Ask them to read the journal entry on the blackline master to pinpoint the place Clark might have been describing in the journal entry.

Remind students that the journal entry is a primary source. This means it has been copied exactly as it was written, including spelling, capitalization, and punctuation. Then read the journal entry aloud to students as they follow along. This should help minimize the decrease in comprehension which the primary source might cause.

If students have trouble determining how to find the location, ask them to scan the paragraph for the most precise or detailed information (Cape Disappointment). Then ask them to identify any directions that are provided with the information about Cape Disappointment, helping them to recognize that knowing the cape is a big clue. Help students work backward from that clue to the "N. and N. E. the coast as as far as my sight Could be extended" clue that helps place Clark likely near present-day Fort Stevens Park.

Activity 3 Water Boundaries   30 minutes

Materials: Blackline Master: Water Boundaries, other maps

Assign students a partner, or have them choose their own.

Distribute the blackline master **Water Boundaries,** which shows the present-day state and national boundary lines.

Tell students to make observations about how the boundaries of various states are alike (many have straight lines and square corners) and different (some have strange jagged borders). Ask students to discuss how the boundaries might have been established in each case.

As pairs come to the realization that jagged boundaries between two areas often follow some kind of natural feature, ask them to brainstorm which features might be represented by these boundaries (rivers, lakes, and oceans). Have students highlight these on their blackline master, and use other maps to identify some of the major bodies of water they highlighted.

Activity 4 Gather Map Sources 30 minutes

Materials: Student Activity Mat 1A United States, online maps, print maps from the Library Media Center (enough for each student to use more than one)

Ask students to review several physical maps from those you provide, as well as those they can find online and Student Activity Mat 1A United States. Ask them to make a list of the different ways that landforms are represented on these maps, and to identify the landforms.

Have students bring one or two of the maps they studied to a small group discussion and show the way their maps represented landforms. Ask a representative from each group to summarize the similarities the group noticed. Point out to students that they will need to use some of these same markings on the maps they will soon create.

Materials: Blackline Master: Around the Nation

Distribute the blackline master **Around the Nation,** which shows climate data for the entire United States. Tell students they will play an "Around the World" style game called "Around the Nation," using clues you share and the information in the blackline master to answer questions more quickly than their opponent.

"Around the World" games begin with one student "traveling" to another student's desk, where both receive a question. The first player to answer the question correctly "travels" to the next opponent's desk while the student who did not win the face-off sits in the first seat. The first student to travel "around the world" and back to their own desk wins.

Ask students questions that require them to analyze the climate data and the geography of the United States, such as "What is the average temperature in northern Florida?" and "Which state whose northern border is partially a river has an average March temperature in the 30s?"

STEP 3 Complete the *Quest*

Part 1 Make a Map ⏱ 60 minutes

Materials: Blackline Master: Make a Map, poster board or art paper, drawing and coloring supplies

Distribute the blackline master **Make a Map**. Read the instructions with students and ensure they understand all the items their map must contain. When students have created their map, display them all together and allow students time to examine each other's maps. They will enjoy seeing the similarities between the maps as well as the ways certain pieces of information were interpreted very differently.

Part 2 Answer the Compelling Question ⏱ 15 minutes

After students create their maps, encourage them to reflect on what they learned. As a class, discuss the compelling question for this Quest: "How do the geographical features of a place make it unique?"

Describe what students have learned and what they should think about. Remind students that they have learned how mapmakers tell us about an area by describing it in terms of landmasses, important bodies of water, its boundaries with other areas, and its climate. They should use what they learned to answer the compelling question.

Become a CARTOGRAPHER

A new piece of land has been discovered by a team of international explorers! It is being divided into three pieces, each belonging to one of the nations who sent explorers. You have been asked to be a cartographer, or mapmaker, and create the first official maps of the new land based on the journal entries of the explorers.

Your Mission:

Study different kinds of maps to learn what kinds of information maps can provide. Then create a map showing the borders, geography, and climate of the new land.

To create your map:

Activity 1 **Tracking Lewis and Clark:** Use clues from Lewis and Clark's journals to trace the route they took to the Pacific Ocean.

Activity 2 **History Detectives:** Try to decode the exact location where Lewis and Clark saw the Pacific Ocean.

Activity 3 **Water Boundaries:** Explore how bodies of water are shown on maps.

Activity 4 **Gather Map Sources:** Collect several maps and compare them with your group.

Activity 5 **Around the Nation:** Play a fun classroom game to test your knowledge of maps!

Complete Your Quest

Use information in the explorers' journal entries to create a map of the new land.

Tracking Lewis and Clark

Read the selection from an undated journal entry written by William Clark. Then use the details in the journal entry to mark Lewis and Clark's proposed route on Student Activity Mat 1A United States.

Use different colors or different kinds of lines (solid and dashed/dotted) to show which parts of the route would be by water and which parts would be by land.

Use the map scale to help you estimate where the proposed trading post might have been, too.

> The <u>rout</u> which I should propose to carry on this trade across the <u>Continant</u> is from St. Louis by the Missouri to the Falls of that river 2575 Miles then by land on horses to the Forks of Kooskooske West of the Great rocky mountains 340 Miles thence Down Lewis River & the Columbia 640 Miles to the Pacific <u>Ocian</u>. The best Situation for a <u>Tradeing</u> Establishment on that River is 125 miles above it's ⟨mouth⟩ Enterance at the ⟨Enterance⟩ **confluence** of Multnomah River from the South
>
> —William Clark, *undated journal entry*

Vocabulary

rout = route

Continant = continent

Ocian = Ocean

Tradeing = trading

confluence, *n.,* the joining of two rivers

Fun Fact

On their journey, Lewis and Clark described about 180 plants and 120 animals that were unknown to scientists at the time.

History Detectives

Read this journal entry from explorer William Clark, looking for clues that will reveal where Lewis and Clark were when they saw the Pacific Ocean for the first time. You will probably need the help of a print atlas or an online map. When your group thinks you know the location, work together to draw an outline map of the area, marking landmasses and water for reference. With your teacher's help, observe the similarities and differences between your group's map and those of other groups.

January 8, 1806

. . . from this point I beheld the grandest and most pleasing prospects which my eyes ever surveyed, in my <u>frount</u> a boundless Ocean; to the N. and N. E. the coast as as far as my sight Could be extended, the Seas <u>rageing</u> with <u>emence</u> wave and <u>brakeing</u> with great force from the rocks of Cape Disapointment as far as I could See to the N. W.

—William Clark, *journal entry, January 8, 1806*

Vocabulary
_____

frount = front
rageing = raging
emence = immense
brakeing = breaking

Fun Fact

It took Lewis and Clark one year, six months, and one day to reach the Pacific Ocean.

Water Boundaries

Study the boundaries on the United States map. Notice that not all boundaries look alike. Work with a partner to discuss how the boundaries are different, and share your ideas about why the boundaries might have been placed where they are.

Use a blue crayon or colored pencil to color the places on the map that you and your partner think might represent water.

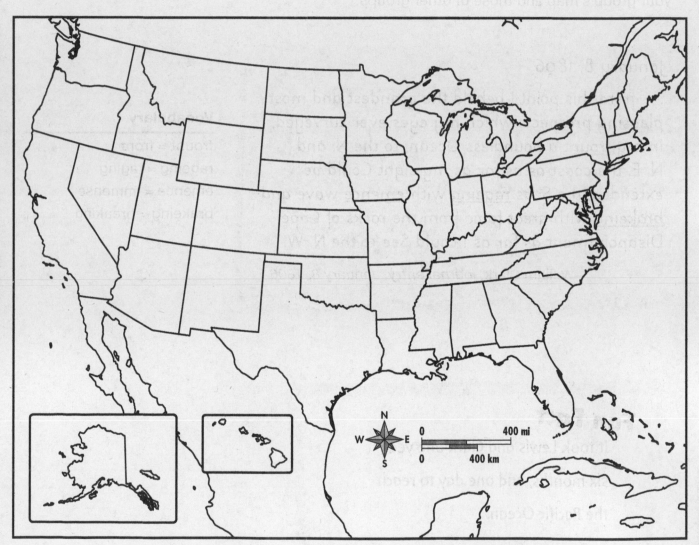

Activity 5

Name _____ Date _____

Around the Nation

Use the information in the map to answer questions your teacher asks as you play a class game.

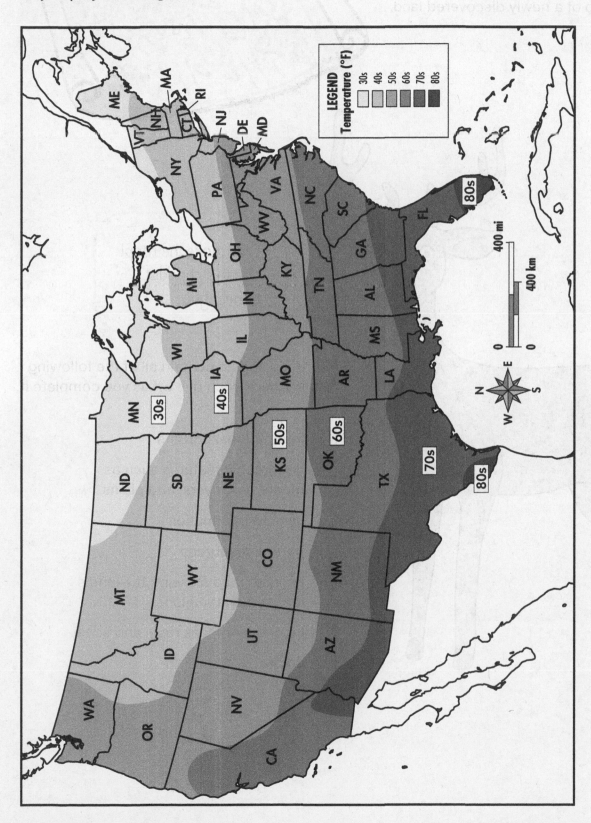

11 Quest Student Worksheet

Quest Findings

Make a Map

Use the journal entry from a team of international explorers to create the first map of a newly discovered land.

Let's make the map! Use this checklist to help you.

Your map should contain all of the following items. Check each one off as you complete it.

- ☐ international borders
- ☐ geographic features such as mountains, rivers, and plains
- ☐ climate information
- ☐ natural resources
- ☐ an inset map showing the land's location on the globe
- ☐ legend, compass rose, and scale
- ☐ color

July 25

We completed our survey of the new land yesterday. Although my fellow explorers and I had no trouble dividing the territory into equal sections for each of our three nations, we are unable to agree upon a name for the landmass as a whole, and we hope the cartographer will be able to assign one.

The land is a great island located about halfway between Japan and the United States in the northern Pacific Ocean. It is shaped a bit like a thick boomerang, or a wide upside-down V. It is approximately 600 miles wide from west to east. At its thickest point, in almost the exact center of the landmass, the island stretches about 200 miles from north to south. It tapers to less than 50 miles across from north to south at its southwestern and southeastern tips.

Japan will lay claim to the western third of the land, since that portion is closest to Japan, and the United States will occupy the eastern third, since that section is closest to the United States. Russia's claim is the middle third and northernmost part of the island.

The climate of this land is much the same whether you are in the southwestern section belonging to Japan or the north central section belonging to Russia, with a couple of exceptions. Most of the island enjoys wet, mild winters and hot, dry summers. However, the high mountain peaks along the northern coast of New Russia have a colder, wetter winter and cooler summers.

The flat plains and temperate climate of New Japan, along with the Placid River running through the territory, make it an ideal spot for agriculture. We have found several citrus and nut crops native to the island. Granite is New Russia's most important natural resource, though some quartz may also be a resource. The forested Jade Hills of New United States make wood its most significant natural resource, and we have found some gold in the Piney River that runs north and south through New United States. The Pacific Ocean is naturally a great source of seafood for all regions.

13

Landforms Matching

Partners, Whole Class ⏱ **20 minutes**

Materials: Index cards, dictionaries, online geography resources

Have students work in pairs to find the definition for a landform you assign (mountain, hill, mesa, plain, plateau, canyon—multiple pairs will be assigned the same landform). Give each pair two index cards, asking them to write the landform name on one card and make a drawing next to it. Then write the definition on the other card. Have paired students representing each landform share the definition they found.

Collect all the index cards, shuffle, and distribute randomly so each student has a card. Tell students to find someone holding the card that matches the one they are holding and sit down together. So, a student holding "mesa" needs to find one of the cards that has a definition close to "like a hill, except the top is flat and not rounded."

When all students are seated again, designate six areas of the classroom and ask all students with the same landform to assemble in their assigned area. Have them compare definitions to ensure everyone found the right match.

If time allows, repeat so students can learn a different landform.

Water Cycle Collage

Individual ⏱ **30 minutes**

Materials: Blackline Master: Water Cycle Collage, glue, scissors, construction paper

Visit https://www3.epa.gov/safewater/kids/flash/flash_watercycle.html and https://water.usgs.gov/edu/watercycle-kids.html so students can explore the water cycle in more detail on their own.

Afterward, distribute the blackline master **Water Cycle Collage** and ask students to cut the components apart and reassemble them on construction paper into an accurate water cycle.

Ask students to discuss what kinds of precipitation are common in their area and how this might be similar to and different from other areas.

Climatologist in Training

Materials: Leveled Readers, paper, pencil, online resources

Leveled Readers for this chapter *(Our Weather, Weather, How Weather Works)* will be useful tools for students as they are introduced to this activity.

Based on what they know about weather, climate, and geography, have students record their educated guesses about the climate where you live. Ask them to guess what the average temperature in certain months is, how much annual rain or snow the area gets, what the average humidity is at certain times, and more.

Consult local records or online sources like https://gis.ncdc.noaa.gov/ to see if anyone's guesses were close.

Ask students how the climate of their area might be unique compared to other areas.

Resources Word Search

Materials: Blackline Master: Resources Word Search, crayons, highlighters, or colored pencils

Distribute the blackline master **Resources Word Search.** Instruct students to find the resources hidden in the word search, but tell them they must circle them using either blue, red, or green, depending on what kind of resource it is.

When students have finished, make a list as a class showing which words fit in each category:

Natural Resources (blue):
coal
gold
lumber
soil

Human Resources (red):
doctor
farmer
teacher

Capital Resources (green):
camera
computer
shovel

16

Update a Song

Materials: Primary Source: Update a Song, online geography resources, encyclopedias from the Library Media Center

Have students rewrite the lyrics to the first verse (or two) of "This Land Is Your Land" by Woody Guthrie to highlight the five geographic regions and a feature of each one.

Begin by playing a recording of the song for students. Discuss the phrases in the song that reference a particular area (California, New York island, redwood forest, Gulf Stream waters). Tell students that these locations are found in a specific geographic region (Northeast: New York island; Southeast: Gulf Stream waters; West: California, redwood forest). Point out that Woody Guthrie did not list any features of the Midwest or the Southwest regions in the song.

Then instruct students to modify the lyrics so that the places referenced are Northeast, Southeast, Midwest, Southwest, and West and all are included. They should also mention a feature of that area, so for example, "From the Midwest wheat fields to the Southwest deserts."

If students need help identifying the regions, have them go online to research which states are in each region. For features of each region, an encyclopedia from the Library Media Center may be a more efficient source than searching online.

Have volunteers give a live or video performance.

Students aware of other patriotic songs or poems they would prefer to update should have the freedom to adapt the activity accordingly.

ELL Support for English Language Learners

Writing To the extent possible, encourage students to imagine new lyrics to the song independently, providing scaffolded support when they are ready to write their ideas down.

Entering: After discussing what lyrics they would like to write, write students' dictated lyrics at the bottom of the page, leaving one blank in place of a key word per line for them to fill in with your assistance.

Emerging: After discussing what lyrics they would like to write, write the first half of each line of students' dictated lyrics at the bottom of the page, leaving the second half of each line for them to fill in with your assistance.

Developing: After discussing what lyrics they would like to write, provide individual line-by-line support as needed while students write the first stanza. Have them write the second stanza providing students with assistance as needed.

Expanding: After students write their lyrics unassisted, have them trade papers with another student to check for accuracy of grammar and spelling.

Bridging: Challenge students to write rhyming lyrics or to add a third new stanza.

Water Cycle Collage

Cut out the pieces along the dotted lines. Use what you have learned about the water cycle to glue the labels onto the illustration to complete the water cycle.

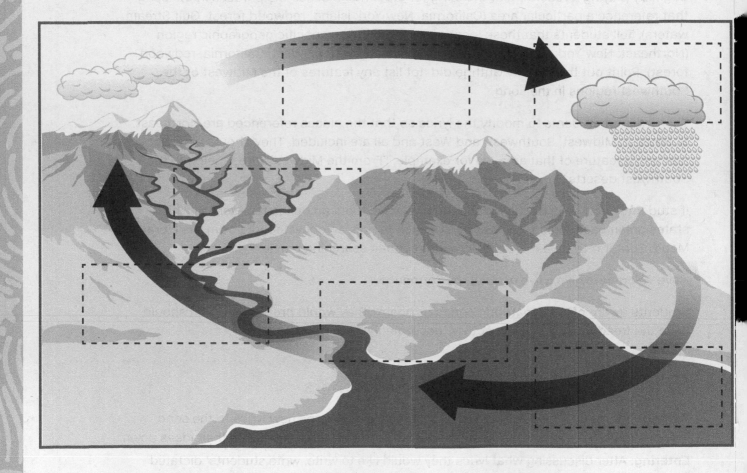

Condensation Water vapor cools and forms drops.	**Lake**	**Evaporation** Water changes to water vapor.
Clouds	**Stream**	**Precipitation** Rain or snow falls.

Resources Word Search

Circle the resource words in the grid as you find them, using the colors indicated based on whether they are a natural resource, a human resource, or a capital resource.

Natural resource—blue

Human resource—red

Capital resource—green

K	K	B	Z	K	D	F	Q	A	J	S	S	Z	L	Y
S	M	I	E	N	L	A	X	Y	X	W	R	U	O	O
R	C	D	S	R	O	R	Z	V	Q	G	M	I	T	J
R	R	M	M	X	G	M	H	G	L	B	J	O	K	Y
E	N	U	A	O	P	E	A	I	E	A	N	F	B	O
T	J	L	G	S	A	R	O	R	N	K	I	W	X	T
U	D	H	O	N	Y	S	R	S	J	T	P	B	C	P
P	L	O	C	Q	F	P	D	Q	C	A	M	E	R	A
M	G	A	C	L	E	V	O	H	S	T	C	X	R	I
O	H	K	O	T	F	V	Q	K	R	M	Z	E	N	A
C	R	W	P	C	O	S	X	K	Q	Y	H	N	A	P
V	U	M	O	F	E	R	A	D	H	C	V	U	C	V
G	Q	G	J	O	Z	Q	Z	M	A	C	W	Y	C	L
T	T	J	M	G	T	K	P	E	M	K	N	H	J	F
Y	P	Z	Y	J	X	Q	T	R	E	S	Z	R	M	B

CAMERA   COAL   COMPUTER   DOCTOR   FARMER

GOLD   LUMBER   SHOVEL   SOIL   TEACHER

Update a Song

Read these lyrics to the famous song "This Land Is Your Land."

"This Land Is Your Land"
By Woody Guthrie

This land is your land This land is my land
From California to the New York island;
From the redwood forest to the Gulf Stream waters
This land was made for you and me.

As I was walking that ribbon of highway,
I saw above me that endless skyway:
I saw below me that golden valley:
This land was made for you and me.

Now, update the lyrics to this song so it mentions a feature of all the geographic regions of the United States: Northeast, Southeast, Midwest, Southwest, and West.

_____

_____

_____

_____

_____

_____

Carlos, Jesse, Marcus, Sam, and Sofia have been friends since second grade. Tomorrow, Sofia is moving from Newport, Rhode Island, to Boston, Massachusetts, to live with her grandmother.

The Parts

5 players:

- **Carlos**
- **Jesse**
- **Marcus**
- **Sam**
- **Sofia**

Director's Notes:

Five friends are gathered in the school cafeteria, eating their last lunch together before Sofia moves away.

Sam: I'm so sad you're moving tomorrow, Sofia. Newport Elementary won't be the same without you!

Sofia:
a little sad
Thanks. I'm going to miss you guys, too.

Marcus: Are you scared, or excited?

Sofia: Both, but mostly scared. I hope I make new friends easily in Boston. So many kids! My grandma says my new school is over twice the size of this one, and I have to ride the subway, or the T as it is also called, to get there! I've never been on a subway!

Jesse: Yeah, not knowing your way around a big urban area can be scary, but at least you won't have to worry about finding new friends.

Carlos: It was a lot harder for me when I had to move from a big city like Philadelphia to rural Pennsylvania when my dad got his first teaching job. Our nearest neighbor lived three miles away, and I had to ride the bus 15 miles to school!

Sofia: Hmmm. I guess that's true. I should at least have plenty of neighbors and friends in Boston. But everything is going to be so different!

Marcus: Different? You haven't moved somewhere different until you've moved from Florida to Colorado—in the winter!

Carlos:
with awe in his voice
Wow! You win! That's a more extreme change than moving between urban and rural areas!

Marcus: Definitely. It took me months to get used to things when the military transferred my mom to Colorado Springs. I went from wearing shorts on a crowded beach to hiking through the snow within a week!

Sam:
smugly
Well, if it's a contest, I think moving to an entirely different country makes my sister the winner.

Carlos: Not so fast, Sam. It was London, England, wasn't it?

Sam: Yep. Different time zone. Different country. Everything different.

Carlos:
doubtfully
I don't think moving from a suburban area in one temperate climate to an urban area in a temperate climate sounds all that much different.

Sam: London gets a LOT more rain than we get, though!
Carlos and Sofia laugh.

Jesse: If it's a contest, Sam, I think my dad is the winner. Try moving from Nova Scotia to remote parts of Ecuador!

Sofia:
embarrassed

I'm not sure I know where either of those places is . . .

Marcus:

I'm pretty sure Ecuador is somewhere on the equator, from the sound of its name.

Jesse:

Right! In South America. A tropical climate. My father went there as part of the Doctors Without Borders program. He lives in Halifax, Nova Scotia, a pretty big city in Canada. It's very close to Maine.

Sofia:

Yeah, I wouldn't exactly call Maine a tropical climate, so that's a pretty dramatic change!

Sam:

Fine, Jesse. You win. [*She pauses a moment.*] But it DOES rain a lot in London!

The children erupt into laughter.

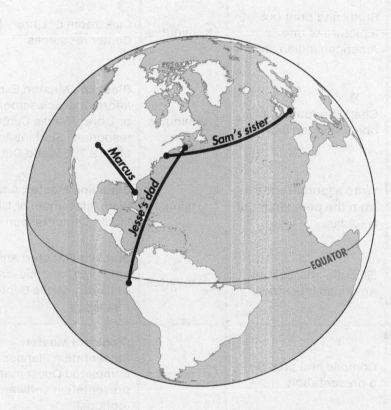

Objectives

- Identify attributes of American Indian nations.
- Draw the route of a European explorer.
- Study the role that American soldiers have played in shaping U.S. and world history.
- Recognize the contributions of American workers to American society.

Quest Project-Based Learning: Historical Presentation

	Description	Duration	Materials	Participants
STEP 1 Set the Stage	Read a blackline master as an introduction to the project.	15 minutes	**Blackline Master:** Quest Kick Off	Whole Class
STEP 2 Launch the Activities	Divide students into consistent small groups.	5 minutes	**Leveled Readers:** *The Story of the Pilgrims; All Aboard the* Mayflower; *The Story of the* Mayflower	Whole Class
Activity 1 American Indian Nations	Study and print out a picture of one American Indian nation.	20 minutes	Classroom or Library Media Center resources	Small Groups
Activity 2 European Explorers	Chart the route(s) of one European explorer.	20 minutes	**Blackline Master:** Explorer Information, classroom or Library Media Center resources, Student Activity Mat 5B The World Outline	Small Groups
Activity 3 American Soldiers	Write a journal entry from the perspective of a soldier.	25 minutes	**Blackline Master:** America's Wars, classroom or Library Media Center resources	Small Groups
Activity 4 American Workers	Fill out a chart about American industries.	25 minutes	**Blackline Master:** American Industry Chart, classroom or Library Media Center resources	Small Groups
STEP 3 ELL Complete the Quest Prepare Your Presentation	Compile and prepare a presentation.	40 minutes	**Blackline Master:** Presentation Planner, completed Quest materials, presentation software (optional)	Small Groups
Deliver a Presentation	Present to the class.	45 minutes		Small Groups
Answer the Compelling Question	Discuss the compelling question.	15 minutes		Whole Class

	Description	Duration	Materials	Participants
Famous Americans Timeline	Sequence famous Americans in time and place.	20 minutes	**Blackline Master:** Famous Americans, Student Activity Mat 3B Time and Place	Partners
Primary Source: Migrant Mother	Study and discuss an image from the Great Depression.	20 minutes	**Primary Source:** Migrant Mother	Small Groups
Civil Rights Letter ELL	Read a book about the civil rights movement and write a letter to the editor.	30 minutes	*Who Was Rosa Parks?* by Yona Zeldis McDonough and Nancy Harrison, or other grade-level civil rights book	Individual
U.S. History Matching Game	Create and play a matching game based on United States history.	15 minutes	Index cards	Partners
Columbian Exchange Vote	Try to determine the origins of items involved in the Columbian Exchange.	15 minutes		Whole Class
Readers Theater: American Students in Europe	Perform a brief skit about American students living overseas.	30 minutes	**Readers Theater:** American Students in Europe	Small Groups

Project-Based Learning: Historical Presentation

Q^{Compelling}**uestion** ## What does it mean to be an American?

Welcome to Quest 2, Historical Presentation. In this Quest, your students will study different groups of Americans. Their study will allow them to compile a presentation about the variety of people who have called America home, followed by an opportunity to discuss the compelling question at the end of this inquiry.

Objectives

- Identify attributes of American Indian nations.
- Draw the route of a European explorer.
- Study the role that American soldiers have played in shaping U.S. and world history.
- Recognize the contributions of American workers to American society.

STEP 1 Set the Stage ⏱ 15 minutes

Begin the Quest by distributing the blackline master **Quest Kick Off**. It will bring the world of the Quest to life, introducing a story to interest students and a mission to motivate them.

Story

The history museum at which your students are volunteering wants to put together a presentation about Americans through the years. They need someone to research and prepare the presentation for younger students.

Mission

Students have been commissioned by the museum to create a presentation about the history of Americans.

STEP 2 Launch the Activities

The following four activities will help students prepare for their presentation by introducing them to Americans from many walks of life. Note that all four can be done independently of the larger Quest.

Assign the appropriate Leveled Reader for this chapter. Divide students into small groups that will remain consistent for all the activities.

Activity 1 American Indian Nations (20) minutes

Materials: Classroom or Library Media Center resources

Explain that the first Americans were here long before European explorers discovered North America, and that there are many different American Indian nations who both lived and still live in various places throughout what is now the United States.

Assign one of the following American Indian nations to each group: Nez Perce, Navajo, Cheyenne, Shawnee, Iroquois, Cherokee.

Provide the groups with classroom or Library Media Center resources, and direct them to look up their assigned nation. Have them print out a picture of the group. Emphasize that they can use either historical or modern imagery, but they should take care to accurately and respectfully represent their assigned nation.

Have students take notes about the group they have been assigned that they would want to use in their presentations, such as where the group is located, or was historically located. Close the activity by discussing some of the present-day contributions of American Indian nations.

Activity 2 European Explorers (20) minutes

Materials: Blackline Master: Explorer Information, classroom or Library Media Center resources, Student Activity Mat 5B The World Outline

Distribute the blackline master **Explorer Information**, which is a resource for students to record information about a European explorer.

Explain that starting with Columbus in 1492, European interest in the Americas grew, and many Europeans led both sea and land expeditions to explore this land that was new to them.

Assign each group one of the following European explorers: John Cabot, Hernando de Soto, Francisco Vásquez de Coronado, Samuel de Champlain, James Cook.

Using classroom or Library Media Center resources, have students look up their assigned explorer, and record the explorer's route(s) on Student Activity Mat 5B The World Outline.

Then have students fill in the additional information about their explorer on their handout, and write a short paragraph to use in their presentations.

Activity 3 — American Soldiers 25 minutes

Materials: Blackline Master: America's Wars, classroom or Library Media Center resources

Explain that America has often had a strong military presence in the world, and that our soldiers have often been important contributing members of our society.

Distribute the blackline master **America's Wars**, which gives information on some of the military conflicts that U.S. troops have fought in.

Have each group select one of the conflicts listed on the handout. Explain that they will be writing a journal entry from the perspective of a soldier in the conflict they have chosen, and that they will need to include at least two facts about the specific conflict in their journal entry. Provide classroom or Library Media Center resources for students who wish to research the conflict further. When students are finished writing, give them an opportunity to edit and revise their work.

Activity 4 — American Workers 25 minutes

Materials: Blackline Master: American Industry Chart, classroom or Library Media Center resources

Explain that American workers are the backbone of American society, and that there are many industries in which the American people work.

Distribute the blackline master **American Industry Chart**, which is a chart that students will fill in concerning different American sectors and industries.

Briefly explain what each industry entails, and then ask students to use classroom or Library Media Center resources to find more details about the industries listed. Have students write one to two sentences about each industry in the spaces provided in the chart.

Part 1 Prepare Your Presentation 🕐40 minutes

Materials: Blackline Master: Presentation Planner, completed Quest materials, presentation software (optional)

Explain that each activity the groups have made will be one point in their presentation. Distribute the blackline master **Presentation Planner** to each group. Have the groups organize their presentations using the planner. If desired, allow students access to presentation software, and assist them in setting up a digital presentation. Have students prepare an appropriate introduction and conclusion to their presentation.

....

ELL **Support for English Language Learners**

Writing Make sure students have access to their completed Quest materials. Support students as they prepare for their presentation.

Entering: Have students work in pairs to list three words that describe the picture printed out during Quest Activity 1. Encourage students to use these written words in their presentation.

Emerging: In small groups, have students study the picture printed out during Quest Activity 1 and write a sentence about what it shows. Have students use this written sentence in their presentation.

Developing: Have students work in small groups, and review the Quest Activity 4 blackline master. Have them choose two industries, and write two sentences to compare and contrast them. Have students include their written sentences in their presentation.

Expanding: Have each student review the Quest Activity 3 blackline master for background information. Then have them write a short paragraph on how the soldiers' experiences might have been similar and different in any given conflict. Encourage students to exchange with a partner in order to make suggestions for revisions. Have students include their revised work in their presentation.

Bridging: Have students work in pairs to write a short summary of what the completed Quest materials show about American life over the years. Have students include this summary as the conclusion for their presentation.

Part 2 Deliver a Presentation minutes

Have groups take turns giving their presentation. Groups should pass around their prepared materials (or use presentation software) and speak about the topics in the order listed on their planners.

If desired, a younger class can be invited to view the presentations as well. After each group has finished, the class can discuss what they liked about each presentation, and what they learned.

Part 3 Compelling Question minutes

After students complete their presentation, encourage them to reflect on what they learned. As a class, discuss the compelling question for this Quest, "What does it mean to be an American?"

Students have learned about many different kinds of Americans. They should think about the attributes of each person or group that they studied. They should use what they learned to answer the compelling question.

Name _____   Date _____

Historical Presentation

The history museum at which you've been volunteering wants to help younger students learn about different groups of Americans. They need someone to research and put together a presentation about the American people.

Your Mission

Create a presentation about the variety of people who have called America home. You will work in small groups to research a variety of Americans. Then, your small groups will present!

To prepare your presentation:

Activity 1 **American Indian Nations:** Study and print out a picture of an American Indian nation.

Activity 2 **European Explorers:** Research one of the North American explorers and draw the route this explorer took.

Activity 3 **American Soldiers:** Study some of the U.S. military conflicts, and write a journal entry from a soldier's perspective.

Activity 4 **American Workers:** Research American industries and complete a chart about American jobs.

Complete Your Quest

Give a presentation about Americans throughout history.

Activity 2

Explorer Information

Fill in the information about your assigned explorer. Draw a picture of the explorer or of the land that was explored. Then write a short paragraph to use in your presentation.

Explorer Name: _____

Areas Explored: _____

Dates of Exploration: _____

_____

_____

_____

_____

_____

_____

_____

_____

_____

_____

_____

Americans and Their History   **32**   Quest Student Worksheet

America's Wars

American soldiers have fought bravely both on American and foreign soil. Read the information about some of the military conflicts America has fought in, and select two facts about one of these conflicts to include in your journal entry.

American Revolution (1775–1783): This first of America's wars was fought in order to gain independence from the rule of Great Britain. The colonial army, led by George Washington, ultimately defeated the British.

American Civil War (1861–1865): This war was fought when Southern states declared they were leaving the Union because they wanted to keep enslaved people. They formed their own country, the Confederacy. The Northern states disputed their right to do so, and America's soldiers fought each other until the Southern generals surrendered in 1865.

Spanish-American War (1898): The United States went to war with Spain following the sinking of the ship, the U.S.S. *Maine.* The resulting American victory led to Spain's loss of control of Cuba, Puerto Rico, the Philippines, and other islands.

World War I (1914–1918): Starting in Europe and expanding due to a complicated series of treaties, World War I threatened the security of Europe and the world. The United States joined the war in 1917, and the Allies (including Great Britain and the United States) won in 1918.

World War II (1939–1945): The most widespread war the world has ever seen, World War II impacted nearly every country in the world. After the bombing of Pearl Harbor, Hawaii in late 1941, the United States joined with Great Britain and Russia to ultimately defeat the Axis powers in 1945.

Name _____ Date _____

American Industry Chart

Fill in the chart using the information you find during your research. Write one or two sentences describing each kind of industry.

Agricultural	_____ _____ _____
Services	_____ _____ _____
Educational	_____ _____ _____
Industrial	_____ _____ _____
Technological	_____ _____ _____
Research/Science	_____ _____ _____

Name _____ Date _____

Presentation Planner

Use this worksheet to plan your presentation. Write a short introduction to your presentation. Write the name of each part of American history that you will talk about, and add notes concerning the points you will make for each. Then, write a short conclusion to your presentation.

Introduction: _____

_____

_____

1. _____

_____

_____

_____

2. _____

_____

_____

_____

3. _____

_____

_____

_____

4. _____

_____

_____

_____

Conclusion: _____

_____

_____

Quick Activities

Famous Americans Timeline

Partners (20) minutes

Materials: Blackline Master: Famous Americans, Student Activity Mat 3B Time and Place

Explain to students that Americans have made many cultural, scientific, and political contributions to the world, and that there have been many Americans who are internationally famous because of their achievements.

Distribute the blackline master **Famous Americans**, which gives information about some famous Americans.

Using Student Activity Mat 3B Time and Place, have students work as partners to mark the dates of birth of each person featured on the handout. Then have them mark a location that the person is known for, using the information on the handout.

Primary Source: Migrant Mother

Small Groups (20) minutes

Materials: Primary Source: Migrant Mother

Explain that at the beginning of the 1930s, the world was enveloped in an economic depression, leading to very high levels of poverty and unemployment.

Distribute copies of **Primary Source: Migrant Mother,** which shows a photograph of a mother and her children affected by the Depression taken by photographer Dorothea Lange.

In small groups, have students review the image, and read the provided information. Then have students discuss the questions on the handout. Circulate to provide support, and review the questions as a class once each group has finished their discussion.

Civil Rights Letter

Individual 30 minutes

Materials: Classroom copies of *Who Was Rosa Parks?* by Yona Zeldis McDonough and Nancy Harrison, or other grade-level civil rights book

Give students some background information about the dawn of the civil rights movement in the mid-1950s, including the role that the *Plessy* v. *Ferguson* court case had in maintaining racial segregation.

Then have students read *Who Was Rosa Parks?*, or another grade-level civil rights book. Review the content as a class. Then have each student imagine living at the time of the civil rights movement. Direct them to write an opinion letter to a fictional newspaper, explaining why they think all Americans should have equal access to all public services. If desired and if time permits, have students trade letters and revise their work based on peer feedback.

Ⓔ Support for English Language Learners

Writing Be sure each student has a copy of the book chosen for the activity. Support students as they practice their writing skills.

Entering: Have each student draw a picture based on something in the book that is *unfair*. Encourage students to write a caption for their drawing.

Emerging: In pairs, have students write a simple sentence explaining one thing in the book that is *unfair*.

Developing: Have each student write two sentences about one thing in the book that is *unfair*, and why it is unfair.

Expanding: In pairs, have students identify three things in the book that are *unfair*, and have them write several sentences explaining why, and what should be done differently.

Bridging: Have students identify three things in the book that are *unfair* and write a paragraph explaining why, what should be done differently, and how their ideas will help make that issue right.

U.S. History Matching Game

Materials: Index cards

Divide students into pairs, and hand out 12 index cards to each pair.
Read the following United States history terms and definitions out loud,
or write them on the board:

- **Columbian Exchange:** The exchange of plant life, animals, technology, and other resources between the Americas and Europe and Asia.

- **American Revolution:** A war fought by the American colonists to win independence from Great Britain.

- **U.S. Constitution:** A document containing the most fundamental laws of the United States.

- **Manifest Destiny:** A term referring to an attitude of superiority and inevitability of United States expansion, usually at the expense of American Indian nations or other indigenous people.

- **American Civil War:** A conflict over the spread of slavery between the Northern and Southern states of the United States.

- **Great Depression:** A time of worldwide economic hardship after the stock market crash of 1929.

Direct students to work with their partners to write each term on one
card, and each definition on another. Students should have 12 cards.
Review each of the terms and definitions and answer questions to ensure
comprehension.

Next, have partners turn all of the cards facedown, and play a matching
game. Students make a successful match if they find both a term and its
corresponding definition. Have them continue until all of the cards have
been used.

Columbian Exchange Vote

Whole Class ⏱ 15 minutes

Review the Columbian Exchange. Then explain that many of the plants and animals that are familiar to Americans have their origins in Europe, and many plants and animals that have their origins in America have become popular in Europe as well.

Write the following plants and animals on the board:

Corn

Apples

Wheat

Turkeys

Potatoes

Chocolate

Cows

Students will try to guess where each item originated: North America or Europe. For each item on the list, hold a vote, and tally the results next to the item's name. Once the votes have been tallied, reveal the origins of each item (as listed in the Answer Key) and see how well your students guessed.

At the end, hold a class discussion to review that plants and animals were not the only things that were exchanged, but that diseases were also passed along. The spreading of new diseases caused a great deal of suffering and death among American Indians, who did not have any immunity built up to the diseases of Europe.

Famous Americans

Read the profiles of some famous Americans. Then use the
information given to complete the timeline and the map.

Date of Birth: January 17, 1706

One of the Founding Fathers of the United States, **Benjamin Franklin** was known for his inventions and for publishing the *Pennsylvania Gazette,* a popular Philadelphia-based newspaper in colonial times.

Date of Birth: around 1788

A Shoshone woman who joined the famed Lewis and Clark expedition while they rested at a fort near North Dakota, **Sacagawea**, also spelled **Sacajawea**, helped to guide the group through the uncharted west.

Date of Birth: April 5, 1856

Born into slavery in Virginia, **Booker T. Washington** became an African American community leader, speaker, and author.

Date of Birth: July 24, 1897

An advocate for women's rights, **Amelia Earhart** was living in New York when she made her famous first solo transatlantic flight.

Date of Birth: December 12, 1915

An award-winning singer and actor from New Jersey, **Frank Sinatra** became an American icon whose career spanned decades.

Migrant Mother

The Great Depression of the 1930s was made worse by the fact that much of the farmland of the Great Plains had become damaged from soil erosion. This caused enormous dust storms and ultimately led to failing crops. The failure of the crops meant that many people who depended on farmwork for a living were suddenly without a means of supporting themselves. Groups of migrant workers would travel around looking for farms that still needed labor in order to feed their families.

Dorothea Lange was a photographer employed by the U.S. government. She took many photographs during the Depression era, including this one of a migrant mother named Florence Owens Thompson and three of her seven children. Study the photograph, then discuss the questions with your group.

Discussion Questions:

• How do you think the mother in the picture is feeling?

• What parts of the picture indicate that the family is poor?

• What do you think Lange was trying to convey about this family, and about the Depression as a whole?

American students living overseas discuss what they miss about the United States.

The Parts

4 players:

- **Emma**
- **Noah**
- **Isabella**
- **Jackson**

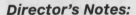

Director's Notes:

Emma, Noah, Isabella, and Jackson are all American students whose parents are working in the United Kingdom. They meet outside of a restaurant.

Emma:	Hi Isabella! Thanks for meeting us here. It's nice to get to know someone else from the U.S.
Isabella: *waving*	Hi Emma! Hi Noah! Did you order yet?
Noah: *grinning*	Yep—French fries for everyone!
Jackson: *walking up to the group*	I think you mean "chips," since that's what they call them here. And, I brought the ketchup!
Noah:	Wow, you did! I've gotten used to having malt vinegar on my fries like everyone else here, but I'll have some ketchup this time.
Emma:	Well, that's one thing *I* don't think I'll ever get used to. Pass the ketchup, please!
Isabella: *looks confused*	Wait, what do you mean, malt vinegar? I haven't ordered fries here before. Do you mean they serve malt vinegar with them instead of ketchup?

Emma: That's right. Noah may like it, but I'll take ketchup any time. And don't forget: order "chips" if you're looking for fries. What *we* call "chips," they call "crisps."

Isabella: Wow, that's different . . . I've only been here for a little more than a week, so I'll need to get used to how they do things here in the U.K. What else is different? What should I know?

Jackson: Well, you've probably already noticed the driving differences here . . . they drive on the opposite side of the road here as they do in the U.S.

Isabella: Yes, I did notice that. It will take some getting used to. I guess that's one difference between the U.S. and Europe.

Noah: Actually, all of the other European countries drive on the right side, too, just like in America; it's just the U.K. that you need to adjust to the difference.

Jackson: Right. We've been on day trips to a lot of European countries at this point. They're all actually quite different from one another.

Noah: I can think of another difference, and it's an important one. You're going to have to get used to the metric system.

Emma: That's right—it took me a while to get used to measuring only in centimeters and kilograms. And don't forget temperature! They use Celsius here. A 70-degree Fahrenheit day in the U.S. is a 21-degree Celsius day here. The weather reports might seem confusing for a while until you learn it.

Isabella:
scratches her head

Yikes, I guess so . . . it seems like there's a lot that's unfamiliar here.

Emma: Yeah, there is. It's exciting to experience new things, but sometimes I miss things the way they are at home.

Noah:	I don't remember the United States as well as Emma does since she's older, so she remembers more from before our move. But we used to live in Colorado, and I remember driving through the mountains. There are mountains here, but not like the Rocky Mountains in Colorado. I remember them being enormous.
Jackson:	I lived in southern California, and the climate is a lot different. I used to go surfing with my cousins all the time. That's something I miss doing.
Isabella: *looks sad*	Honestly, I think I'll miss my family the most. We have a big family, and we've all lived in New England for as long as anyone can remember. This is a big change for me.
Emma: *tries to be cheerful*	That can be hard. I communicate a lot with people back home using e-mail. Noah and I both talk on the phone with our grandparents a lot, too.
Jackson:	I also talk to people back home a lot. But I've also made a lot of friends here, too. And I like that I can experience cultures that aren't mine. It helps me to appreciate the United States all that much more!
Isabella: *starts to smile*	Actually, that's a really nice way to think about the situation. Thanks, Jackson.
Jackson:	No problem. But for right now, I think we should eat these fries before they get cold.
Noah:	I think you're right. Let's get to it. Who wants ketchup, and who wants vinegar?
Isabella: *smiling*	I'll try the vinegar. After all, I am living in the U.K. . . . but keep the ketchup handy. Just in case.

Objectives

- Describe local, state, and federal officeholders, their duties, and how to contact them.
- Understand what services are provided by different branches and levels of government.
- Contrast the civil and criminal court systems and track a federal court case.
- Learn how a bill becomes a law.
- Study a constitutional amendment.

Quest Project-Based Learning: Prepare to Be President

	Description	Duration	Materials	Participants
STEP 1 Set the Stage	Read a blackline master as an introduction to the project.	15 minutes	**Blackline Master:** Quest Kick Off, Student Activity Mat 4B Quest	Whole Class
STEP 2 Launch the Activities		5 minutes	**Leveled Readers:** *We Are America; Being American; Our America*	Whole Class
Activity 1 Who's in Charge?	Collect information about government officials.	35 minutes	**Blackline Master:** Who's in Charge?, classroom or Library Media Center resources	Small Groups
Activity 2 Where Do I Go to Get Things Done?	Look up government services.	20 minutes	**Blackline Master:** Where Do I Go to Get Things Done?, classroom or Library Media Center resources, completed Quest materials from Activity 1	Small Groups
Activity 3 What Can They Do for Me?	Contact an elected representative.	30 minutes	Completed Quest materials from Activity 1, computers with e-mail access or paper letter-writing materials	Small Groups
Activity 4 How Do Courts Work?	Compare and contrast civil and criminal courts.	20 minutes	Compare and Contrast graphic organizer, classroom or Library Media Center resources	Small Groups
Activity 5 Local Government Field Trip (optional)	Visit a local government office.	3 hours		Whole Class
STEP 3 ELL Complete the Quest Make a Who's Who in Government Booklet	Compile information about federal, state, and local government officials.	1 hour 30 minutes	Completed Quest materials; computers, printers (for physical publication); class or school Web page (for electronic publication)	Small Groups
Answer the **Compelling Question**	Discuss the compelling question.	15 minutes		Whole Class

	Description	Duration	Materials	Participants
What Government Can Do	Look up what different levels of government can do.	20 minutes	Student Activity Mat 3A Graphic Organizer, classroom or Library Media Center resources	Individual
Primary Source: Law of the Land **ELL**	Discuss the Twenty-Sixth Amendment.	15 minutes	**Primary Source:** Law of the Land	Whole Class
Complete an Infographic	Research how a bill becomes a law.	30 minutes	**Blackline Master:** How a Bill Becomes a Law	Small Groups
Free Speech and School	Discuss *Tinker* v. *Des Moines Independent School District*.	20 minutes	**Blackline Master:** Tracking a Court Case	Whole Class
Readers Theater: Vote for School Board	Perform a short skit about the candidates for a district's school board.	30 minutes	**Readers Theater:** Vote for School Board	Small Groups

Project-Based Learning: Prepare to Be President

 **Compelling Question** Who makes decisions that matter to your community?

Welcome to Quest 3, Prepare to Be President. Your students are planning to run for president in the 2060s. This Quest will help them get to know what local, state, and federal offices they could run for to prepare for the presidency. They will research different offices, find out who holds them, and prepare a Who's Who in Government booklet. Their study of government will help them to discuss the compelling question at the end of this inquiry.

Objectives

- Describe the local, state, and federal officeholders, their duties, and how to contact them.
- Understand what services are provided by different branches and levels of government.
- Contrast the civil and criminal court systems and track a federal court case.

STEP 1 Set the Stage ⏱ 15 minutes

Begin the Quest by distributing the blackline master **Quest Kick Off.** It will bring the world of the Quest to life, introducing a story to interest students and a mission to motivate them. Also, use Student Activity Mat 4B Quest to have students track their learning as they complete their Quest. At this point, they should fill in the first box, "Quest Topic."

Story

Your students are planning to run for the presidency in the 2060s. They will need to hold various state, local, and federal offices to get to the top. They can start now by researching these offices.

Mission

Students will make a Who's Who in Government booklet showing the names and job descriptions of state, local, and federal officials in all three branches of government.

STEP 2 Launch the Activities

The following five activities will help students prepare to publish their booklet by guiding them through a process of learning about government roles and offices. Note that Activity 5: Local Government Field Trip, is optional. It is not counted towards the total time for the Quest and does not appear on the students' **Quest Kick Off** blackline master. However, it is recommended that this activity be included in the Quest if possible.

You may assign the appropriate Leveled Reader for this chapter.

Activity 1   Who's in Charge?   (35) minutes

Materials: Blackline Master: Who's in Charge?, classroom or Library Media Center resources

Copy and distribute the blackline master **Who's in Charge?** You will probably need to give two or more copies to each student. Alternatively, each member of a group may record a different portion of the information.

Have students use classroom or Library Media Center resources to look up the names of people elected from your area. First, help students look up a variety of elected officials in your town, city, or county. These may include city councilors, a mayor or town manager, county commissioners, or judges. Then, have students research their state representative and state senator. Finally, have students research their representative in Congress and your state's two federal senators.

Have students record the information they collect on their blackline master.

If students are using Internet resources, encourage them to look for Web sites ending in .gov Some examples are:

- www.senate.gov
- www.house.gov

If Internet resources are not available, have students refer to the government services section of the local phone book.

After students have gathered the information, review the job titles with them. Ask about the responsibilities of the people in each of the listed jobs. Correct any misconceptions, and explain the functions of jobs that are new to the students.

Activity 2 — Where Do I Go to Get Things Done? 20 minutes

Materials: Blackline Master: Where Do I Go to Get Things Done?, classroom or Library Media Center resources, completed Quest materials from Activity 1

Distribute the blackline master **Where Do I Go to Get Things Done?** Read the instructions with students and check that they understand the task.

Students may have collected some of the information needed to answer the questions in Activity 1. Suggest places where they can look up answers to the questions. In each case, point out the level of government involved: federal, state, or local. Some of the government Web sites where students can find information are as follows:

Driver's license: Find the Web site for your state's Department of Motor Vehicles. (Note that your state may delegate DMV duties to your local government.)

Downed-tree-branch removal: phone book (local level)

Register a new business: Find the Web site for registering a new business in your state.

Get a United States passport: www.travel.state.gov (federal level)

Activity 3 — What Can They Do for Me? 30 minutes

Materials: Completed Quest materials from Activity 1, computers with e-mail access or paper letter-writing materials

In this activity, students will investigate the services provided to constituents by their state and federal legislative representatives. Define the term *constituent* as "any person who lives in the representative's district." Point out that although students are too young to be voters, they are constituents.

Divide students into two groups. Have one group contact the office of your local state representative. Have the other group contact the U.S. congressional representative's office. Instruct students to use e-mail or write a letter asking what services the office provides to citizens and constituents.

Activity 4 How Do Courts Work? (20) minutes

Materials: Compare and Contrast graphic organizer, classroom or Library Media Center resources

Explain that courts apply the laws in two kinds of cases: criminal cases, in which a crime has been committed, and civil cases, in which there may not be a crime, but there is a disagreement that cannot be resolved by the people involved.

Distribute the Compare and Contrast graphic organizer. Have students look up ways in which the two court systems are alike (e.g., both use judges and juries) and different (e.g., criminal courts can set prison sentences, civil courts can make people pay damages).

Internet resource on this topic include:

• judiciallearningcenter.org/student-center

Activity 5 Local Government Field Trip 3 hours

This activity is optional and is not included on the student Quest Kick Off page or included in the number of sessions or total time for the Quest.

To prepare for this activity, make arrangements with your local officials to take students to visit a local government office, such as the mayor's office, city hall, a council meeting, or county or municipal court. If possible, have students meet with officials from one or more of the branches of government.

Have students prepare questions in advance. Coach them in how to address the officials they will meet. For example, introduce them to the custom of calling a mayor *Mr. Mayor* or *Madam Mayor.*

On the day of the trip, have students bring note-taking materials and take notes of the answers to their questions.

After the trip, have students write thank-you letters to the officials who met with them.

Part 1 Make a Who's Who in Government Booklet 1 hour ⏰ 30 minutes

Materials: Completed Quest materials; computers, printers (for physical publication); class or school Web page (for electronic publication)

Guide students in compiling the information they have gathered into a Who's Who in Government booklet showing the names and job descriptions of federal, state, and local officials in all three branches of government.

Encourage and guide students to work collaboratively by dividing up the necessary tasks:

• Writing
• Fact checking
• Illustrating
• Proofreading
• Cover design for the booklet

Students can complete this portion in multiple sessions if necessary. Encourage students to send a copy with a thank-you note to anyone outside the classroom who helped with the Quest.

⬤ELL **Support for English Language Learners**

Writing Support students in organizing their Who's Who in Government booklets by offering support with categorizing the officials they researched. In addition, encourage interested and able students to use appropriate technology to communicate in writing the information they have collected.

Entering: Write the following category heads on the board: *Federal, State,* and *Local.* Say the name of one of the officials the students researched and have students come up and write an *F, S,* or *L* based on what category the official is in.

Emerging: Create a three-column chart on the board with the following category heads: *Federal, State,* and *Local.* Ask students to come up to the board and fill in the names of the officials they researched.

Developing: Hand out two copies of a three-column chart. On the first copy, ask students to write the category heads *Federal, State,* and *Local* and then fill in the names of the officials they researched. Then have them fill in the second copy by recategorizing the officials by their branch, using the following heads: *Executive, Legislative,* and *Judicial.*

Expanding: Ask students to work together in pairs and practice using technological tools. Have pairs create in a word processing program a three-column table with the headings *Federal, State,* and *Local* and have them type in the names of the officials they researched.

Bridging: Ask students to work individually and practice using technological tools. Have pairs create in a word processing program a three-column table with the heads *Federal, State,* and *Local* and have them type in the names of the officials they researched. Then have them create another three-column table with the heads *Executive, Legislative,* and *Judicial* and have them recategorize the names of the officials.

After students complete their booklets, encourage them to reflect on what they learned. As a class, discuss the compelling question for this Quest: "Who makes decisions that matter to your community?"

Remind students of what they learned about the three branches of government. Have them consider the influence that each branch has in their community. Remind them to think about what decisions are made at the federal, state, and local levels. They should use what they learned to answer the compelling question.

In addition, have students fill in the rest of the boxes on the Student Activity Mat 4B Quest.

★★★★★★★★★★★★★★★★★★★★★★★★★★★★★★

Prepare to Be PRESIDENT

You are planning to run for president in the 2060s. You will want to run for local and state offices first to gain experience. To help you get started, learn about current elected officials and what they do.

Your Mission

Start your career in public service by making a Who's Who in Government booklet. The booklet should show the names and job descriptions of state and local officials in all three branches of government so you know what offices you can run for to prepare to be the U.S. president.

★★★★★★★★★★★★★★★★★★★★★★★★★★★★★★

To gather information for your booklet:

Activity 1 **Who's in Charge?:** Look up the elected officials whose actions affect the place where you live.

Activity 2 **Where Do I Go to Get Things Done?:** Discover what parts of government provide some everyday services.

Activity 3 **What Can They Do for Me?:** Write to your representative in Congress and in the state legislature about the services their offices provide.

Activity 4 **How Do Courts Work?:** Explain how courts in your community apply the law.

Complete Your Quest

Create and publish your booklet to government officials.

Who's in Charge?

Name	Title	How to Contact	Office Location

Activity 2

Where Do I Go to Get Things Done?

Citizens sometimes need to talk to different government officials to complete everyday tasks. For each of the given situations, look up whether you would need to work with the local, state, or federal government to complete the task. Write down the name of the specific office or Web site you would contact.

Situation 1: You are old enough to drive and want to apply for a driver's license.

_____

_____

_____

Situation 2: A tree branch has fallen down in a storm and is blocking your street.

_____

_____

_____

Situation 3: You need a license to open your new business.

_____

_____

_____

Situation 4: You are applying for a United States passport.

_____

_____

_____

Quick Activities

What Government Can Do
Individual (20) minutes

Materials: Student Activity Mat 3A Graphic Organizer, classroom or Library Media Center resources

Distribute the Student Activity Mat 3A Graphic Organizer. Have students write *What Government Can Do* at the top and then label the three boxes *Local, State,* and *Federal.*

Have students look up and record in the organizer actions that can be taken by the different levels of government. Encourage students to express these actions using verbs. Answers will vary and may include:

- Federal government: Declare war, make treaties, regulate interstate commerce, conduct foreign policy, issue passports
- State level: License drivers, license businesses, police highways
- Municipal, county, or local level: Issue building permits, tax property, oversee public health

Some answers are correct for more than one level of government. For example, all three levels may levy taxes, legislate, and have a police force.

Primary Source: Law of the Land
Whole Class (15) minutes

Materials: Primary Source: Law of the Land

Distribute copies of **Primary Source: Law of the Land,** which includes the text of Article VI, Clause 2 of the United States Constitution (known as the Supremacy Clause) and the Twenty-Sixth Amendment.

Read the Supremacy Clause aloud and help students to interpret it. Ask: *What does this clause say about the relationship between state governments and the national government?* (The Supremacy Clause gives the U.S. Constitution the final legal authority over the states.)

Next, read the Twenty-Sixth Amendment aloud with students and ask: *What would happen if our state decided to make a state law that only people over 25 could vote?*

Support for English Language Learners

Reading Distribute **Primary Source: Law of the Land** to students. Support their understanding of the basic meaning of the text and any unfamiliar words.

Entering: Write unfamiliar words from the text on the board, such as *pursuance, treaties, authority,* and *abridged*. Say the words aloud, point to them, and define them. Then have students read them aloud as you point to them.

Emerging: Write unfamiliar words from the text on the board, such as *pursuance, treaties, authority,* and *abridged*. Say the words aloud, point to them, and define them. Ask students to read the words with you and tell the words' definitions in their own words as you point to them.

Developing: Write unfamiliar words from the text on the board, such as *pursuance, treaties, authority,* and *abridged*. Say the words aloud, point to them, and define them. Then, as you point to each word, have students read the word and use it in a sentence.

Expanding: Write unfamiliar words from the text on the board, such as *pursuance, treaties, authority,* and *abridged*. Say the words aloud, point to them, and define them. Then, as you point to each word, have students read the word, tell its definition in their own words, and use it in a sentence.

Bridging: Ask students to take turns reading sections of the blackline master aloud. Have them paraphrase the meaning of what they read in their own words.

Complete an Infographic

Small Groups minutes

Materials: Blackline Master: How a Bill Becomes a Law

Explain that an infographic uses words, illustrations, and graphics to show information. Infographics are especially useful for showing the steps in a particular process, as in this example about how a bill becomes a law.

Distribute the blackline master **How a Bill Becomes a Law.** Explain that these steps describe how a bill can become a federal law.

Ask students to work in small groups and research how a bill becomes a law in the United States Congress. Then, they should cut out the steps at the bottom of the page and paste them into the correct boxes in the infographic. Tell students that each step will be used once and only once.

Free Speech and School

Materials: Blackline Master: Tracking a Court Case

Begin with a basic introduction to the court system. Ask: *Why would someone need to go to court?* Listen to student answers, then explain that someone might need to go to court because he or she had been accused of a crime and had become a defendant in a criminal case. The person could have a disagreement with a neighbor or in a business transaction that could not be resolved. This would make the person either a plaintiff (the one who takes the case to court) or a defendant in a civil case.

Then explain that if someone who is involved in a court case has reason to believe the court did not hear the case fairly, he or she can appeal the decision to a higher court.

Distribute the blackline master **Tracking a Court Case.** Referring to the diagram, explain that a case can reach the United States Supreme Court either from state courts or from federal court. People appeal cases from lower courts all the way up to the Supreme Court.

Explain that the Supreme Court chooses what cases to hear. It does not have to hear every appeal.

Next, give an overview of the case *Tinker* v. *Des Moines Independent School District.* Tinker was one of a group of students who wore black armbands to school as a silent antiwar protest. She and the other students were suspended. The students' parents sued the school for violating their right to free speech. A United States district court sided with the school principal, but the Supreme Court reversed the district court's decision.

Read the quotation and ask students to consider its meaning. Ask: *How is being at school different from being in another public place, like a park?*

A Supreme Court Justice wrote about the Tinker case:

"The District Court recognized that the wearing of an armband for the purpose of expressing certain views is the type of symbolic act that is within the Free Speech Clause of the First Amendment. . . . First Amendment rights, applied in light of the special characteristics of the school environment, are available to teachers and students. It can hardly be argued that either students or teachers shed their constitutional rights to freedom of speech or expression at the schoolhouse gate."

Primary Source

Law of the Land

Read the excerpts from the United States Constitution that say that the Constitution is the highest law in the land. Then discuss the excerpts with your class. Ask your teacher to define any words or phrases that are difficult for you to understand.

Article VI, Clause 2

This Constitution, and the Laws of the United States which shall be made in Pursuance thereof; and all Treaties made, or which shall be made, under the Authority of the United States, shall be the supreme Law of the Land; and the Judges in every State shall be bound thereby, any Thing in the Constitution or Laws of any State to the Contrary notwithstanding.

Amendment XXVI

Section 1.

The right of citizens of the United States, who are 18 years of age or older, to vote, shall not be denied or abridged by the United States or any state on account of age.

Section 2.

The Congress shall have the power to enforce this article by appropriate legislation.

How a Bill Becomes a Law

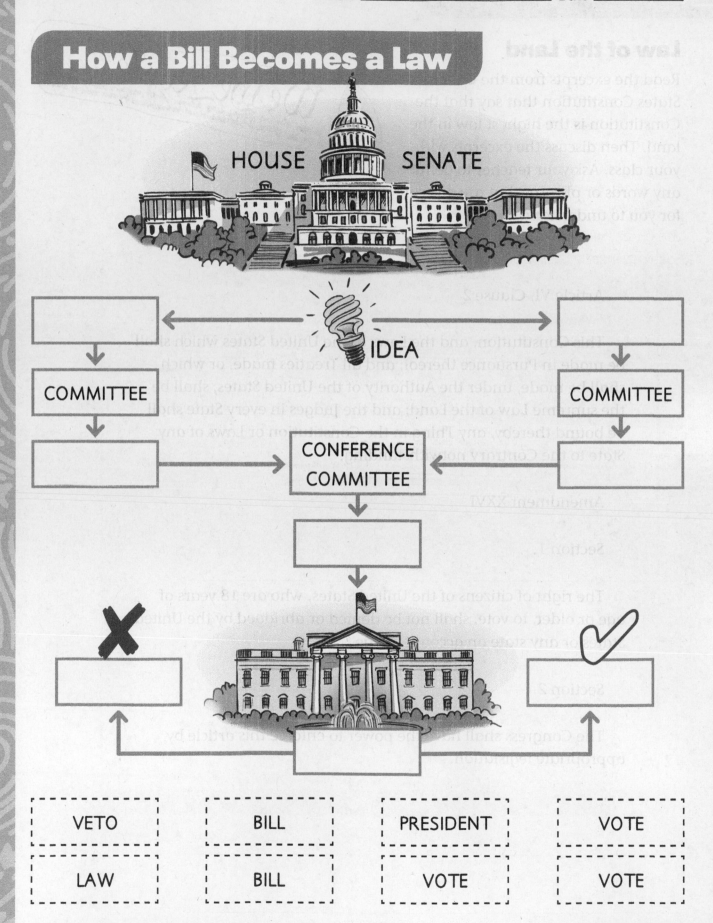

HOUSE   SENATE

IDEA

COMMITTEE   COMMITTEE

CONFERENCE
COMMITTEE

VETO	BILL	PRESIDENT	VOTE
LAW	BILL	VOTE	VOTE

Tracking a Court Case

In the United States, courts operate on a local, state, and federal level. The highest court is the federal Supreme Court, which takes on cases which are very important for the laws of the United States as a whole. A decision that comes from a local or state court can be appealed, but needs to go through several lower courts before it can reach the Supreme Court. Study the chart, which will help you track the path of a court case, such as the case of *Tinker* v. *Des Moines Independent School District*.

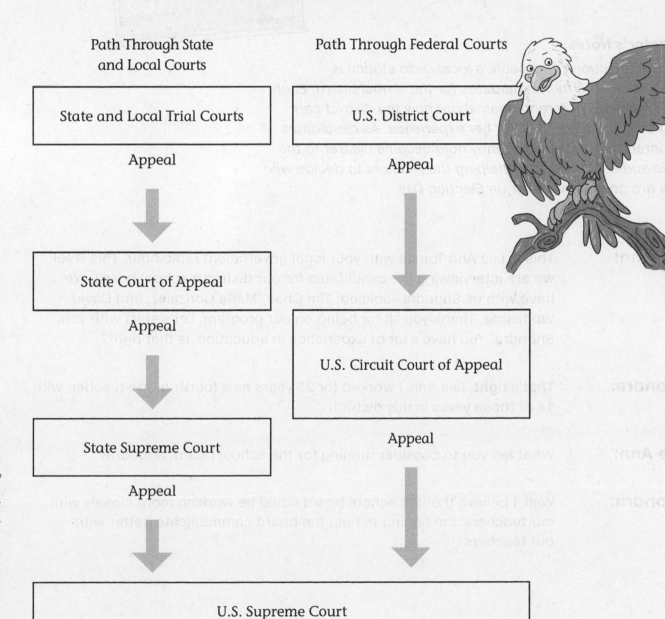

Path Through State and Local Courts

State and Local Trial Courts

Appeal

State Court of Appeal

Appeal

State Supreme Court

Appeal

Path Through Federal Courts

U.S. District Court

Appeal

U.S. Circuit Court of Appeal

Appeal

U.S. Supreme Court

Vote for School Board

A local radio host interviews four candidates for the school board.

The Parts

5 players:

- **Lee Ann Tomita,** radio host
- **Shondra Jackson,** candidate
- **David Whiteside,** candidate
- **Tim Chao,** candidate
- **Maria Gonzalez,** candidate

Director's Notes:

As town elections approach, a local radio station is interviewing the four candidates for the school board. Each candidate has different ideas about how the district can best be run based on his or her experience. As candidates are interviewed, the views they hold become clearer to the radio audience, hopefully helping the listeners to decide who they are going to vote for on Election Day.

Lee Ann:	This is Lee Ann Tomita with your local government radio hour. This week we are interviewing the candidates for our district's school board. We have with us Shondra Jackson, Tim Chao, Maria Gonzalez, and David Whiteside. Thank you all for being on our program. Let's start with you, Shondra. You have a lot of experience in education, is that right?
Shondra:	That's right, Lee Ann. I worked for 25 years as a fourth-grade teacher, with 14 of those years in this district.
Lee Ann:	What led you to consider running for the school board, Shondra?
Shondra:	Well, I believe that the school board could be working more closely with our teachers. I'm hoping to help the board communicate better with our teachers.

Lee Ann: Definitely an important consideration. Now to candidate David Whiteside—David, what led you to run for office?

David: Well, I think Shondra is right. Communication is important, but I also think that this district needs to be looking at ways to cut costs and save the taxpayers money. I worked as a small business owner for over 20 years, and I know how to make good business decisions. I think our district can save money in a lot of ways, and I have some of those ways detailed on my campaign Web site if your listeners want to take a look.

Lee Ann: Thank you, David. Now moving on . . . Tim Chao. What do you think this district needs most?

Tim: Well, I'm a father of three children, and as any parent knows, the most important thing is making sure that kids get a quality education. I have to disagree with David that we should be cutting spending. I think we should be providing more opportunities for our children. We may need to spend more money to provide those opportunities.

David: Absolutely, there's no question about providing opportunities, but I think there are ways that we can cut costs and still give our kids a great education.

Lee Ann: Let me take a moment here to introduce our last candidate, Maria Gonzalez. Maria, how do you feel about the issues facing this district?

Maria: Well it's interesting that we're having a discussion about spending, Lee Ann, because I think that one of the issues with cutting costs is that art and music programs are sometimes seen as less important than math or science, and I'd like to see the district add more art and music to the classroom.

Tim: We have many art and music after-school programs. I don't think we need more classroom time spent on that.

Shondra: Actually, I agree with Maria—last summer I was at a class for teachers, and they told us that kids learn other subjects better when they spend time learning about art and music. I think it builds a sense of community in the school, too.

Tim: I think there has to be a balance, because we don't want art and music to replace time that could be spent on math or science.

Maria: Of course, but if we don't provide art and music in the classroom, we're not doing a good job of helping students to become well-rounded citizens.

Lee Ann: We're having a great discussion here about education in our district, but we're almost out of time, and we have to go to a commercial break. Can each of you give our listeners a final message? David, can we start with you?

David: Sure, I'm the candidate who can help the district to run more efficiently and save the taxpayers money.

Lee Ann: Tim?

Tim: Our district needs to emphasize quality, and I will work hard to make sure all of our kids get the quality education every parent wants for their child.

Lee Ann: Maria, how about you?

Maria: I'm looking to provide our students with access to many subjects, including the arts, which I think we need more of in this district.

Lee Ann: And finally, Shondra?

Shondra: No matter who you vote for, please get involved in the community. Our district needs to hear from everyone so we can work together and do what's best for our kids.

Lee Ann: And that's all we have time for. Thank you to our four school board candidates. We'll be right back after this short break.

Objectives

- Classify goods and services as wants or needs.
- Explain how advertisers use incentives to attract customers.
- Identify techniques used in advertisements.

Quest Project-Based Learning: Create an Advertisement

	Description	Duration	Materials	Participants
STEP 1 Set the Stage	Read a blackline master and an introduction to the project.	15 minutes	**Blackline Master:** Quest Kick Off	Whole Class
STEP 2 Launch the Activities	Make relevant connections and build content background for the Quest.	5 minutes		Whole Class
Activity 1 What Am I?	Classify items as needs or wants and goods or services.	20 minutes	Index cards or construction paper, markers	Small Groups
Activity 2 ELL Brainstorm	Make a list of favorite goods and services.	15 minutes	**Blackline Master:** Brainstorm	Individual
Activity 3 Incentive Idea	Create a coupon or sales flyer for a favorite good or service.	30 minutes	**Blackline Master:** Incentive Idea, crayons or colored pencils	Partners, Individual
Activity 4 **Primary Source:** Analyze an Advertisement	Examine a vintage advertisement.	20 minutes	**Primary Source:** Analyze an Advertisement, markers, highlighters	Individual, Whole Class
Activity 5 Collect Sample Ads	Collect and share effective advertisements.	20 minutes	Magazines, newspapers, classroom or Library Media Center resources	Individual, Whole Class
STEP 3 Complete the Quest Create an Advertisement	Create an advertisement for a favorite good or service.	60 minutes	Various art and audio/visual materials (poster board, markers, crayons, colored pencils, construction paper, video camera, audio recording device), classroom or Library Media Center resources	Individual
Deliver a Presentation	Students display or play their advertisement.	30 minutes		Whole Class

| Answer the Compelling Question | Discuss how advertisements affect the decisions we make. | (15) minutes | | Whole Class |
| Quest Reflection | Summarize the Quest activities and findings. | (5) minutes | Student Activity Mat 4B Quest | Individual, Whole Class |

Quick Activities

	Description	Duration	Materials	Participants
Charades	Play a game to learn about producers and consumers.	(20) minutes	Student Activity Mat 2A Personal Finance Tips	Partners, Whole Class
Bartering and Currency	Role-play to understand the importance of currency.	(15) minutes	Teacher-created sentence strips; word cards; classroom object like a checker or play coin	Small Groups, Whole Class
Supply and Demand	Role-play to see supply and demand in action.	(30) minutes	**Blackline Master:** Supply and Demand; classroom items like pencils, stickers, and books; water fountain passes, computer passes, free homework pass	Whole Class, Small Groups
Opportunity Cost	Calculate the opportunity cost of a good not purchased.	(10) minutes	**Blackline Master:** Opportunity Cost	Individual
Imports and Exports ELL	Investigate classroom items to learn where they were made.	(20) minutes	T-Chart graphic organizer, Leveled Readers: *Our Economy*; *The Nation's Economy*; *The Global Economy*	Individual, Small Groups, Whole Class
Readers Theater: Divide and Conquer	Perform a brief skit about brothers and sisters using division of labor.	(30) minutes	**Readers Theater:** Divide and Conquer	Small Groups

Project-Based Learning: Create an Advertisement

Compelling Question

How do advertisements affect the decisions we make?

Welcome to Quest 4, Create an Advertisement. In this Quest, students will study how producers and consumers interact with the economy and how advertisements play a role in consumer purchasing. They will use what they learn to create an advertisement of their own, which will prepare them to discuss the compelling question at the end of this inquiry.

Objectives

- Classify goods and services as wants or needs.
- Explain how advertisers use incentives to attract customers.
- Identify techniques used in advertisements.

STEP 1 Set the Stage ⑮ minutes

Begin the Quest by distributing the blackline master **Quest Kick Off.** It will bring the world of the Quest to life, introducing a story to interest students and a mission to motivate them.

Story

Tell students to imagine they have written an online review of a product that went viral. The review was eventually seen by the company that creates the product; the company has contacted students to ask if they would help come up with ideas for a new marketing campaign.

....

Mission

Students must create a convincing advertisement for a product or service they love, featuring a monetary incentive.

Students have some flexibility on this project; they can create the advertisement in any format they choose. If they choose a television commercial or radio advertisement, they will need to record or at least perform the commercial live for their final project.

STEP 2 | Launch the Activities

The following five activities will help students prepare for creating their advertisement by helping them learn more about advertising and incentives. Note that all five can be done independently of the larger Quest.

As you begin, give students an opportunity to build content background as a launch into the following activities. Ask students what they know about advertisements and how they relate to the economy.

Activity 1 **What Am I?** **minutes**

Materials: Index cards or construction paper, markers

Remind students that a *need* is something a person requires to live, and a *want* is something that would be nice for a person to have but is not required to live. Then tell them that things people buy can be classified as either *goods* or *services*. A *good* is a product you can buy, but a *service* is something other people do for you. Provide examples of each.

Assign students to groups of four, with each person representing one of the following categories: *want, need, good,* or *service.* Ask each student to write his or her category on an index card or construction paper.

Call out the name of a *good* or *service,* such as a soccer ball or someone performing a health checkup. Have groups come to a consensus on whether the object named is a *want* or a *need,* and a *good* or a *service.* The two students assigned to those characteristics stand to signal the group's answer. In the case of the soccer ball, the students assigned to represent *good* and *want* should rise.

Activity **Brainstorm** **minutes**

Materials: Blackline Master: Brainstorm

Distribute the blackline master **Brainstorm,** which provides guidance in thinking of several possibilities for the advertisement students will create.

Have students brainstorm possible goods or services for the Quest advertisement. They should choose a good or service they like and know something about. Instruct students to fill out the blackline master to start thinking of possibilities.

After students fill in all of the information, have them assign a number ranking to the goods or services in order of preference. As they assign numbers, encourage them to think about not just which goods or services they like best, but which ones they can most easily write and talk about.

Ask students to circle their top choice before moving on.

Support for English Language Learners

Writing Explain to students that advertisements often include strong written statements to attract consumers. Encourage students to practice their writing skills when brainstorming goods and services.

Entering: Have students draw pictures of the goods or services they chose and have them label at least four of their drawings.

Emerging: Have students work with Entering students to label their drawings. Then, have students complete their own lists. Provide coaching for spelling where needed; have students correct mistakes with your assistance.

Developing: After students have completed their own lists, have them write one complete sentence for one good or service listed. Then, encourage students to share their writing with a partner.

Expanding: Have students write three complete sentences for three of the goods and services they listed. Encourage students to share their writing with a partner.

Bridging: After completing the activity, offer students the chance to write a children's book to teach others about wants, needs, goods, and services.

Activity 3 Incentive Idea minutes

Materials: Blackline Master: Incentive Idea, crayons or colored pencils

Discuss types of monetary incentives, such as sales and coupons. Tell students that an incentive is a thing that encourages us to take an action, such as making a purchase.

Explain how a coupon is a piece of paper or digital image that entitles the person holding it to receive a good or service at a special price that is otherwise unavailable. Usually coupons have an expiration date, but not always.

Then explain that a sale is a temporary reduction in the price of a good or service that applies to everyone for a certain period of time. It does not require a coupon. Tell students that sometimes companies take out an ad in a magazine, newspaper, or television commercial so they can offer a coupon or announce a sale.

Have students discuss with a partner the good or service they are planning to use for the Quest, and talk through what kinds of sales or coupons might be effective for buyers. For example, a smoothie stand might offer a buy one, get one free coupon so a consumer can bring a friend, in the hopes that the friend will become a customer, too. A store selling school supplies might have a clearance sale to encourage parents to buy all their children's supplies at the same time.

Distribute the blackline master **Incentive Idea.** Have students create a coupon or sales flyer based on the good or service they will advertise.

Activity 4   Primary Source: Analyze an Advertisement   (20) minutes

Materials: Primary Source: Analyze an Advertisement, markers, highlighters

Distribute **Primary Source: Analyze an Advertisement,** which shows a vintage advertisement that students will analyze.

First, discuss different advertisement formats, such as newspaper, magazine, poster, billboard, radio, television, and Internet. Ask students which format they think this vintage advertisement appeared in, and which formats they think might be most effective now.

Next, review the section that lists techniques used in advertisements. For each technique, ask students to think of examples in ads they have seen. If they can't think of any ads they have seen with the technique, encourage students to make one up.

Then, read the text in the primary source advertisement aloud as a class. When finished, ask students to complete the exercise independently.

Before closing, ask students how this advertisement might have been different if it had appeared in other formats. Ask students who already know what kind of advertisement they will create to share their choices with the class. This could help those struggling to make a decision.

Activity 5   Collect Sample Ads   (20) minutes

Materials: Magazines, newspapers, classroom or Library Media Center resources

Have students browse various forms of print or digital media looking for examples of advertisements they think are effective or appealing. If needed, provide students a list of appropriate, safe Web sites for them to visit. Ask students to share the ads they found with the class, pointing out what features or techniques in particular demonstrate the ad's goal.

STEP 3 Complete the Quest

Part 1 Create an Advertisement (60) minutes

Materials: Various art and audio/visual materials (poster board, markers, crayons, colored pencils, construction paper, video camera, audio recording device, computer), classroom or Library Media Center resources

Instruct students to create the advertisement they have been planning throughout the Quest. Tell them to think about the format they would like to use; some students will prefer to create a print advertisement, while others will prefer to create an audio or visual advertisement. Encourage them to think about the advertising techniques that are most effective in the format they chose. If audio/visual materials are not accessible in the classroom, encourage students to visit the Library Media Center to work with librarians in using audio/visual devices for recording purposes.

Part 2 Deliver a Presentation (30) minutes

Have students who created audio or video advertisements play their creation. Ask audience members to identify techniques the advertisement features. Have those who created a print advertisement show it to the class. Call on volunteers to explain which techniques were used.

Part 3 Answer the Compelling Question (15) minutes

After students create their advertisement, encourage them to reflect on what they learned. As a class, discuss the compelling question for this Quest, "How do advertisements affect the decisions we make?"

Describe what students have learned and what they should think about. Remind students that they have learned about goods, services, wants, and needs, as well as different types of incentives, such as sales and coupons. They should use what they learned to answer the compelling question.

Part 4 Quest Reflection (5) minutes

Materials: Student Activity Mat 4B Quest

Distribute Student Activity Mat 4B Quest and have students fill out the mat to provide closure for the Quest. Ask volunteers to share a few of their responses aloud.

Quest **Kick Off**

Create an Advertisement

Congratulations! Your work has gone viral! A review you recently posted online has received thousands of views, and it has even caught the attention of the company you were reviewing. The company loves your work and wants to know if you will help them create a new advertisement.

Your Mission
Create an advertisement for a good or service you love. You will need to think about how to sell the good or service and who will be your target audience. Then, you can make an effective advertisement!

To create your advertisement:

Activity 1 **What Am I?:** Classify items as *goods* or *services* and *needs* or *wants*.

Activity 2 **Brainstorm:** Make a list of your favorite goods and services in order to write an advertisement for one of them.

Activity 3 **Incentive Idea:** Create a coupon or sales flyer for your favorite good or service.

Activity 4 **Analyze an Advertisement:** Examine a vintage advertisement to understand how advertisements appeal to people.

Activity 5 **Collect Sample Ads:** Collect and share several advertisements you think are effective.

Complete Your Quest

Create an effective, interesting advertisement (fit for newspaper, magazine, online, radio, television, or billboard) for your chosen good or service.

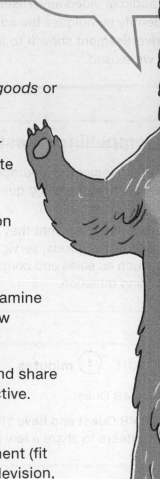

Brainstorm

It is time to start thinking about the good or service you will advertise for your Quest project. To start, think about some of your favorite goods and services. Write down three goods or services for each category.

After you have filled in the information for each category, assign a number ranking to every good or service in that category. Use 1 to rank your favorite pick, and 3 to rank your least favorite pick.

Goods I Need   **Ranking**

_____   _____

_____   _____

_____   _____

Goods I Want   **Ranking**

_____   _____

_____   _____

_____   _____

Services I Need   **Ranking**

_____   _____

_____   _____

_____   _____

Services I Want   **Ranking**

_____   _____

_____   _____

_____   _____

Now look back at all the goods and services, paying attention to the ranking you assigned each one. Determine the good or service for which you will create an advertisement and circle it.

Name _____ Date _____

Incentive Idea

In the space, create a coupon or sales flyer offering a special incentive for buying the good or service you will be advertising.

Analyze an Advertisement

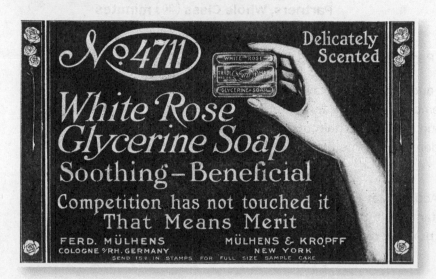

Advertisers use several techniques to encourage consumers to spend money. Some techniques include:

- Convincing consumers that a want is really a need
- Appealing to consumers' emotions or senses
- Making a good or service seem attractive or trendy
- Showing testimonials from other consumers
- Explaining why a good or service is better than the competition's

Study the advertisement on this page. Be sure to read the text as well as review the image. Then, complete the exercise.

Underline in blue the words or phrases that are designed to appeal to consumers' emotions or senses.

Highlight in yellow the words or phrases that show this soap is better than any other soap.

Write an imaginary testimonial from a customer. A testimonial is a statement from a customer telling how he or she uses the product or what he or she loves about it.

_____

_____

_____

Quick Activities

Charades

Materials: Student Activity Mat 2A Personal Finance Tips

Review the definition of *producers* and *consumers*. Have pairs of students create a scenario they can act out which demonstrates an interaction between a producer and a consumer (e.g., a barber giving someone a haircut). Ask the class to guess what the activity is, and which student represents the producer and which represents the consumer.

As a follow-up, distribute Student Activity Mat 2A Personal Finance Tips to pairs of students. Have students put a star next to the box that represents the role of a producer and an arrow next to the box that represents the role of a consumer.

Bartering and Currency

Small Groups, Whole Class 15 minutes

Materials: Teacher-created sentence strips, one per group; word cards to complete each group's sentence strips; classroom object like a checker or play coin

Divide the class into groups. Give each group a sentence strip with a word missing. Also give each group a word card, but make sure that the word does not complete the group's sentence. Keep all the word cards that complete the sentence strips correctly.

Tell the class that groups will need to trade words in order to make complete, coherent sentences. Instruct groups to send a representative to other groups to trade. They will quickly discover they can't help each other. When all groups have had a chance to attempt a trade, but unsuccessfully, ask students to explain what is going wrong. They will by now have figured out that they aren't finding the word they need.

Then tell the class that you can help; you will trade them the word they have in exchange for a "classroom coin," which they can later use to purchase exactly the word they need. This could be a checker, a play coin, or anything at all.

Invite groups up one at a time to exchange their word for your coin. When all groups have a "classroom coin" instead of a word, tell students that your store is now open. Invite representatives to your store one at a time, where they can browse the available words and pay you their coin for exactly the word they need.

Ask students to recap the lesson by explaining how currency changes the way people conduct business.

Supply and Demand

Whole Class, Small Groups ③⓪ **minutes**

Materials: Blackline Master: Supply and Demand; classroom items like pencils, stickers, and books; water fountain passes, computer passes, free homework pass

Have students cut out the currency on the blackline master **Supply and Demand.**

Tell them they can use this currency to purchase two to three classroom items such as pencils, stickers, and books. Allow all students to make their purchases.

The purpose in this first half of the activity is to set up a situation where students no longer have an equal amount of currency before the next part begins. After students have made their purchases, tell them you have a few special items you will offer to the highest bidder.

First, offer a pass to use the water fountain. Tell students the pass is good for one use, and you have 60 (or some appropriately large number, to represent a large supply) of these available. Then, show them a pass for 15 minutes of computer time, and explain there are only five of these available. Finally, offer a free homework pass, noting that there is only one of these available. Add other incentives as you see fit, making sure to create a supply and demand dilemma for the most valuable items by limiting their quantity.

Offer the items for auction, and observe the law of supply and demand in action! The water fountain passes will sell cheaply or possibly not at all, as students save their money for the free homework pass, and the homework pass will sell for the maximum amount of money a student possesses.

Ask students to meet in small groups to summarize how this activity demonstrates supply and demand.

Have students work together to answer the questions on the blackline master **Supply and Demand.**

Opportunity Cost

Materials: Blackline Master: Opportunity Cost

Define *opportunity cost* for students. Remind them that when they choose between two items, the opportunity cost is the value of the item they did not buy. Provide several examples aloud. Then have students complete the blackline master **Opportunity Cost** to calculate actual opportunity cost based on decisions they make.

Imports and Exports   Individual, Small Groups, Whole Class 20 minutes

Materials: T-Chart graphic organizer, Leveled Readers: *Our Economy*;
The Nation's Economy; *The Global Economy*

Distribute T-Chart graphic organizer. Instruct students to label the columns "Imports" and "Exports." Remind students that imports are goods a country or state buys or brings into their territory, and exports are goods a country or state sells or sends out of their territory to another place. Encourage them to think of the word *exit* to help them remember export.

Have students circulate around the classroom, investigating ten classroom items for evidence of where they were made. Show them how to look for "Made in" data on commercially made items. Encourage them to get creative with some of the items they check (their backpacks, classroom furniture, or anything they choose!).

Tell students that if an item says "Made in the United States," they should record its name in the "Exports" column. If an item lists any other country of origin, tell them to list both the item and the country in the "Imports" column.

When students are finished, compile a list as a class and ask students what observations they can make about our country's imports and exports from this activity.

Finally, encourage students to investigate the Leveled Readers *Our Economy*; *The Nation's Economy*; and *The Global Economy.* Ask students who read the same readers to meet in small groups and hold a five-minute discussion on the content.

Support for English Language Learners

Speaking Explain to students that prefixes help to determine word meanings. Tell students that *im-* and *in-* mean "in" and "into" while *ex-* means "out" and "outside." Review imports and exports. Then, have students practice their speaking skills using *im-/ex-* words.

Entering: Make a list of other *im-/ex-* words on the board. Ask students to repeat after you as you read them aloud. Define each word as you go. Encourage students to repeat the definitions.

Emerging: Make a list of other *im-/ex-* words on the board. Ask students to repeat after you as you read them aloud. Define each word as you go. After you have reviewed the list of words and their definitions, begin to name definitions at random. Ask students to call out the word from the list that matches a definition you name.

Developing: Make a list of other *im-/ex-* words on the board. Have students try to determine what the words might mean based on the prefixes. Encourage students to use them in sentences.

Expanding: Ask students to call out words that begin with *im-/ex-* and, as they call them out, list these words on the board. Have students provide definitions for each word they name. If they have trouble, suggest they look in classroom reference materials.

Bridging: Invite students to deliver a brief speech that uses as many *im-/ex-* words as possible. Have listeners make a list of the words used. See who identifies the most *im-/ex-* words.

Supply and Demand

Cut out this paper currency for use in a classroom activity.

1. Explain the law of supply and demand. Use examples from the classroom activity in your explanation.

_____

_____

_____

2. What happens to the price of an item when the supply is low and demand is high?

_____

3. What happens to the price of an item when the supply is high and demand is low?

_____

Opportunity Cost

Your parents give you money to go shopping. You think about buying something you wanted for a long time, but your younger sibling has a birthday coming up.

Choose one item from this list to buy for your younger sibling.

Calculate the opportunity cost of the item on the list that you would have liked to purchase for yourself.

Microscope	$41.00
Video game	$34.00
Trading card game	$19.00
Hardcover book	$12.00
Friendship bracelet kit	$14.00
Magazine subscription	$23.00
Movie poster	$8.00
Stuffed animal	$18.00

1. Which item would you purchase for your sibling?

   _____

2. Which item would you purchase for yourself?

   _____

3. What is the opportunity cost of buying the item for your sibling instead of the item you want?

   _____

Readers Theater
Divide and Conquer

Four siblings are feeling glum because it is a beautiful Saturday morning and they are stuck inside doing chores.

The Parts
6 players:

- **Cameron**, older brother
- **Carly**, older sister
- **David**, younger brother
- **Dawn**, younger sister
- **Mom**
- **Narrator**

Director's Notes:

Action takes place in the family room of the Lopez home. When the play begins, all four children are sitting on the couch looking dejected.

Mom:	I'm sorry, kids. I know it is a beautiful day and you all want to be outside playing, but your responsibilities in this house must come first. You can go outside as soon as everyone's chores are complete. Not before.
Cameron:	Could we at least—
Mom: *sternly*	Cameron!
Cameron:	I know. Okay, Mom. We'll do our chores.
Mom: *sighs*	I'll make you a deal. If each of you will pick up your dirty clothes and take them to the laundry room, empty your trash cans, make your beds, and dust your shelves, I might let you wait until tomorrow on the rest of your chores.
Narrator:	The children look around at each other.

The Nation's Economy

83

Readers Theater

© Pearson Education, Inc., All Rights Reserved

Carly:	Well, it's better than no deal, I guess.
Narrator:	Mom exits the room.
Carly:	It's going to take me all day just to find the floor of my room. I'll never get done!
Dawn:	I wouldn't mind it so much if I didn't have to make so many trips downstairs with all my dirty clothes.
David:	I just can't make myself get up and get started. It is so overwhelming.
Cameron: *rising*	Well, it's not going to get done sitting here.
Narrator:	Cameron begins to exit the room. As he does, he looks down at the newspaper on the coffee table and stops in his tracks. He picks up the newspaper and becomes absorbed in what he sees.
Dawn:	What's wrong, Cameron?
Cameron:	Guys! This advertisement says the school carnival is today! It's starting in two hours!
Carly: *excitedly*	Oh! My teacher is going to be in the dunk tank! I didn't know that was today! I just can't miss that!
David: *taking the newspaper from Cameron and reading the advertisement*	I'd like to see that, and this bounce house looks awesome. I don't see how we're going to have our chores done in two hours, though.
Narrator:	The room is silent and the children sit back down a bit deflated as they realize how difficult the task ahead is.
Dawn:	I have an idea. In social studies class, we learned about this idea called division of labor.
David:	Division of huh?
Dawn: *laughing*	Division of labor. You'll learn about it in fourth grade, too.
Cameron:	Oh! I remember that! It's where people in a company divide up a big task into lots of small tasks, and each person specializes in just one part of it.

Dawn:	Right. My teacher said it speeds up work because people are able to focus on just one thing and get really good at it. And fast!
Carly:	So you mean one of us would do the same job in everyone's room? Like one person would empty all the trash cans, and another person would make all the beds?
Cameron:	Exactly! I call picking up the dirty clothes!
Dawn:	Fine by me. I don't even want to pick up my OWN clothes, much less yours.
David:	I can do everyone's trash. That's easy!
Carly:	I'm the tallest. I'll dust the bookshelves.
Dawn: *thinking for a moment*	I think that leaves me with making the beds. Hmmm. Why does that sound so much easier than cleaning my whole room alone?
Cameron:	Let's go! I bet we could be done before the carnival even starts! David, you could be the first one in the bounce house if we hurry!
Narrator:	The children rush off to complete their jobs. They reassemble in the living room a short time later, breathless but excited. Mom enters the room.
Mom:	There is no way your rooms are clean already. That's impossible.
Carly: *beaming*	It's true! Go check!
Narrator:	Mom exits to go check the children's rooms.
Cameron:	That was the fastest our rooms ever got clean, guys! We should do this all the time!
Narrator:	Mom reenters the room, surprised but happy.
Mom:	Well, what are you all still sitting here for? I hear there's a carnival starting soon!
Narrator:	The children cheer, jump up from the couch, and head happily to the carnival.

Chapter 5 Regions: The Northeast

Objectives

- Label a map of the Northeast to show how much maple syrup each state produces.
- Research facts about sugar maples and the syrup they produce.
- Understand the history of maple syrup production.
- Identify sugar maple trees.
- Use a primary source to understand the importance of Ellis Island.

- Research famous authors who lived in the Northeast region.
- Research events in United States history that occurred in the Northeast region.
- Describe physical features of the Northeast region.

Quest Project-Based Learning: Create a Web Site

	Description	Duration	Materials	Participants
STEP 1 Set the Stage	Read a blackline master as an introduction to the project.	10 minutes	**Blackline Master:** Quest Kick Off	Whole Class
STEP 2 Launch the Activities	Discuss upcoming activities and background information.	5 minutes		Whole Class
Activity 1 Mapping Maples	Label a map of the Northeast region showing state's maple syrup production.	20 minutes	**Blackline Master:** Mapping Maples, Student Activity Mat 2B United States Outline	Individual
Activity 2 Maple FAQ	Research questions about how maple syrup is produced.	35 minutes	**Blackline Master:** Maple FAQ	Individual, Whole Class
Activity 3 ELL The History of Maple Syrup Production	Research the origins of maple syrup.	30 minutes	Paper, pencil, online and Library Media Center resources, books about maple syrup	Individual
Activity 4 Identifying Maple Trees	Learn the characteristics of maple trees and their leaves.	15 minutes	Paper, pencil, classroom and Library Media Center resources	Individual
STEP 3 Complete the Quest Create a Web Site	Use Quest activity materials to assemble a Web site.	60 minutes	Computer, notes taken in Activities 1–4	Individual
Answer the Compelling **Question**	Discuss the compelling question.	15 minutes		Whole Class

	Description	Duration	Materials	Participants
Immigrant Remembers Ellis Island	Read and discuss excerpts from an interview with Nelly Ratner Myers.	20 minutes	**Blackline Master:** Immigrant Remembers Ellis Island	Whole Class
Crossword	Create a crossword about the states in the Northeast region.	30 minutes	**Leveled Readers:** *What's It Like in the Northeast?; Life in the Northeast; Exploring the Northeast*; paper, pencil, research resources	Individual, Partners
Famous Authors From the Northeast	Research the lives and work of famous authors from the Northeast.	20 minutes	**Blackline Master:** Authors From the Northeast	Partners
America's History Timeline	Collaborate to create a timeline of important events that occurred in the Northeast region.	25 minutes	**Blackline Master:** America's History Timeline, online and print research resources, Student Activity Mat 3B Time and Place, butcher paper or poster board	Small Groups
Ode to the Northeast	Write a song or poem about the physical features of the Northeast region.	20 minutes	**Blackline Master:** Ode to the Northeast	Whole Class, Partners
Readers Theater: Fall Foliage Tour	Perform a brief skit about a family on a fall foliage tour in the Northeast.	20 minutes	**Readers Theater:** Fall Foliage Tour	Small Groups

Project-Based Learning: Create a Web Site

Compelling Question
How can a natural resource affect an area?

Welcome to Quest 5, Create a Web Site. In this Quest, your students will research various aspects of the maple syrup industry and create a Web site. As they do their research and create the Web site, they will be preparing to discuss the compelling question at the end of this inquiry.

Objectives

- Label a map to show how much maple syrup each state in the Northeast produces.
- Research facts about sugar maples and the syrup they produce.
- Understand the history of maple syrup production.
- Identify sugar maple trees.

STEP 1　Set the Stage　⏱ minutes

Begin the Quest by distributing the blackline master **Quest Kick Off**. It will bring the world of the Quest to life, introducing a story to interest students and a mission to motivate them.

Story

The fictional Northeast Maple Association is looking for someone to help them put together a Web site about maple production in the Northeast region of the United States.

Mission

Students will create Web site content for the Northeast Maple Association, including maps, FAQs, and illustrations.

STEP 2 Launch the Activities

The following four activities will help students prepare to create their Web site by building their knowledge of sugar maple trees and the maple syrup business. Note that all four activities can be done independently of the larger Quest.

Activity 1 Mapping Maples minutes

Materials: Blackline Master: Mapping Maples, Student Activity Mat 2B United States Outline

The sugar maple tree, also known as the hard maple or the rock maple, is one of several varieties of maple trees. Other varieties include silver maple, striped maple, red maple, bigleaf maple, Japanese maple, and many more. The leaves of sugar maples turn red, yellow, or orange in the fall season, contributing to the beautiful fall foliage for which the Northeast region is known.

Distribute the blackline master **Mapping Maples,** which shows information from a recent Census of Agriculture about how much maple syrup was produced in each state. Students will use the information on the blackline master to color states in the Northeast region on Student Activity Mat 2B United States Outline according to how much maple syrup each state produces. Students will also add a legend to the map to indicate how many gallons of maple syrup are represented by each color.

Remind students that they should use this information when they create the Web site for the Northeast Maple Association.

Activity 2 Maple FAQ  minutes

Materials: Blackline Master: Maple FAQ

Distribute the blackline master **Maple FAQ,** which features six questions about maple trees. Explain to students that FAQ stands for Frequently Asked Questions. Tell them that many Web sites include a page like this to help people find answers to common questions quickly. Instruct students to research the answers to each of the questions and record their answers on the lines. Review answers as a class when students have completed their research.

Materials: Paper, pencil, online and Library Media Center resources, books about maple syrup

Have students research the origins of maple syrup as a Northeastern food, including its use by American Indian nations, who introduced maple sugaring to the pilgrims. Then have students write a short summary of the history in a project journal. Finally, have them include an entry that explains how the maple syrup industry affects the Northeast region. To do this, encourage students to think about businesses and jobs that exist because of maple syrup production. You might even ask them to imagine how the region would be different if the maple syrup industry did not exist or experienced a catastrophic event.

Remind students that they should use this information when they create the Web site for the Northeast Maple Association.

This Web site may be helpful as students research: www.americanmaplemuseum.org and click on "The History of Maple Syrup Production".

● ●

(ELL) Support for English Language Learners

Writing Help students prepare for the About Maple Syrup page of their Web site by instructing them to record their research findings in a project journal.

Entering: Have students illustrate key ideas in the history of maple syrup production. Ask them to write a word or a phrase describing each key idea they have illustrated.

Emerging: Have students illustrate key ideas in the history of maple syrup production. Ask them to write phrases or a simple sentence describing what they drew.

Developing: Have students illustrate key ideas in the history of maple syrup production. Encourage them to write a one-sentence summary under each drawing. Ask them to trade with a partner to review.

Expanding: Have students illustrate at least three key ideas in the history of maple syrup production. Ask them to trade illustrations with a partner, and have each write a short descriptive text explaining each illustration drawn by their partner. Help the partners review each others' text for accuracy.

Bridging: Have students illustrate three to five key ideas in the history of maple syrup production, suggesting that each drawing focus on a different key idea. Then, ask students to write a short paragraph summarizing each of their illustrations. Encourage them to write each paragraph with a focus on a key idea and the details that support that idea.

Activity 4 Identifying Maple Trees ⏱(15) minutes

Materials: Paper, pencil, classroom and Library Media Center resources

Have students study the characteristics of a sugar maple tree. Ask them to draw a picture of a sugar maple leaf in a project journal and label it with a caption that includes a description of the tree.

Remind students that they should use this information when they create the Web site for the Northeast Maple Association.

This Web site may be helpful as students research: www.maine.gov. In the search field, write "maple trees", then click on "Forest Trees of Maine: Handbooks & Guides: Publications" where you can click on the link to "Maples".

STEP 3 Complete the *Quest*

Part 1 Create a Web Site ⏱(60) minutes

Materials: Computer, notes taken in Activities 1–4

Have students create a Web site for the Northeast Maple Association. Remind students that in Activities 1 through 4, they created documents they can use to help build the Web site. Tell them their Web site must include at least a FAQ, an About page (detailing the history of maple syrup production), a map showing the states that produce maple syrup, and a drawing of a sugar maple leaf.

Use the Project-Based Learning rubric to assess students' finished products.

Part 2 Answer the Compelling Question ⏱(15) minutes

After students create a Web site for the fictional Northeast Maple Association, encourage them to reflect on what they learned. As a class, discuss the compelling question for this Quest: "How can a natural resource affect an area?"

Describe what students have learned and what they should think about. Remind students that they have learned about the characteristics of sugar maple trees and the maple syrup they produce, including a study of the history of maple syrup production. They should use what they learned to answer the compelling question.

Create a Web Site

The Northeast Maple Association is looking for someone to help them create a Web site for their organization.

Your Mission
Research sugar maple and maple syrup production to build content for the Web site.

To create the Web site:

Activity 1 **Mapping Maples:** Color a map to show how much maple syrup is produced in different states in the Northeast region of the United States.

Activity 2 **Maple FAQ:** Research the answers to commonly asked questions about maple trees and maple syrup.

Activity 3 **The History of Maple Syrup Production:** Write a short summary of the history of maple syrup production.

Activity 4 **Identifying Maple Trees:** Draw an illustration of a sugar maple leaf.

Complete Your Quest

Use all the documents you created in Activities 1–4 to create four pages on the Web site:

- one page with a map showing which states produce maple syrup
- one page with Frequently Asked Questions
- one page titled "About Maple Syrup" telling the history of maple syrup production and how the maple syrup industry affects the Northeast
- one page titled "About Maple Trees" that shows a picture of a maple leaf and describes a maple tree

Activity 1

Mapping Maples

The Northeast Maple Association would like to create an online map showing how much maple syrup is produced in each state. Use the information in the chart to help create the map.

The chart shows an estimate of how many gallons of maple syrup several states in the Northeast region produced in 2017.

State	Syrup (gallons)
Connecticut	20,000
Maine	709,000
Massachusetts	84,000
New Hampshire	154,000
New York	760,000
Pennsylvania	139,000
Vermont	1,980,000

Northeast Maple Association

Color each state in the Northeast region on Student Activity Mat 2B United States Outline to show how many gallons of maple syrup it produced. Then add this legend to the Student Activity Mat.

Gallons Produced	Color
0 – 50,000	Red
50,001 – 100,000	Orange
100,001 – 500,000	Yellow
500,001 – 750,000	Green
750,001 – 1,000,000	Blue
1,000,001 – 2,000,000	Purple

Name _____ Date _____

Maple FAQ

The Northeast Maple Association needs a page in their
Web site with Frequently Asked Questions (FAQ) to
answer some of their online visitors' questions. This is
a list of the most common questions the organization
receives. Help create the page with FAQ by researching
the answers to each one.

Northeast Maple Association

1. What is maple syrup made from?

_____

_____

2. How is the sap removed from the trees?

_____

_____

_____

3. Does tapping hurt the trees?

_____

_____

4. Why can the syrup only be produced in late winter or early spring?

_____

_____

_____

5. How much maple syrup can be made from each tree?

_____

_____

6. Is pancake syrup the same thing as maple syrup?

_____

_____

_____

Quick Activities

Immigrant Remembers Ellis Island

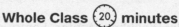 Whole Class 20 minutes

Materials: Primary Source: Immigrant Remembers Ellis Island

Distribute Primary Source: **Immigrant Remembers Ellis Island**, which features excerpts from an interview with Nelly Ratner Myers. Read the content with students and discuss. Ask students to summarize the information and ask what additional questions they have about immigration or Ellis Island.

The National Park Service interviewed Ms. Myers about her immigration experience as part of the Ellis Island Oral History Project, which has collected more than 1,700 immigrant stories. You can learn more about the project and access additional interviews at www.nps.gov and search "Oral histories - Ellis Island".

The full audio version and an edited transcript of the interview with Ms. Myers are also available at www.nps.gov. Write Nelly Rattner Myers in the search field and navigate to "Oral Histories", then click on "audio version" or "edited text version".

Crossword

Individual, Partners 30 minutes

Materials: Leveled Readers: *What's It Like in the Northeast?; Life in the Northeast; Exploring the Northeast* paper, pencil, research resources

Have students create a crossword puzzle with at least eleven words and clues – one for each state. They may include more if they desire. They can include any details about each state they choose. If students need help thinking of something, suggest they find out about natural resources, unusual geographic features, important tourist attractions, and major industries in each state. After they are done creating the crosswords, have students exchange papers with a partner and solve each other's puzzles.

The leveled readers may provide information students can use. Make these available along with other classroom, Library Media Center, and online research options.

Famous Authors From the Northeast

Partners (20) **minutes**

Materials: Blackline Master: Famous Authors From the Northeast, Student Activity Mat 1B United States Outline

Read aloud a poem or two from significant Northeast region poets such as Emily Dickinson ("I'm Nobody! Who are you?") and Robert Frost ("Stopping by Woods on a Snowy Evening"). Tell students these poets are from the Northeast region.

Distribute the blackline master **Famous Authors From the Northeast**. Instruct students to work with a partner to research the state where each author lived and the name of one of their famous works.

Have students map the locations where the author lived on Student Activity Mat 1B United States Outline. If desired, an additional activity might include finding out and mapping the locations of other famous people who are from the Northeast (presidents, singers, actors, athletes).

America's History Timeline

Small Groups (25) **minutes**

Materials: Blackline Master: America's History Timeline, online and print research resources, Student Activity Mat 3B Time and Place, butcher paper or poster board

Distribute the blackline master **America's History Timeline**. Have small groups research events from the founding of the United States which occurred largely in the Northeast region. Assign groups some events from the list.

- French and Indian War
- Boston Tea Party
- Signing of the Declaration of Independence
- British Surrender at Yorktown
- Constitutional Convention

Suggest that students use Student Activity Mat 3B Time and Place to create their own timeline while researching their assigned events. When all groups have finished, invite them to use the butcher paper or poster board to assemble one large timeline. Discuss the timeline as a class, and display throughout the unit.

Ode to the Northeast

Whole Class, Partners ⏱ 20 minutes

Materials: Blackline Master: Ode to the Northeast

Distribute the blackline master **Ode to the Northeast.** As a class, make a list of the types of water shown on the map (rivers, oceans, lakes, bays, sounds, waterfalls). Then list landforms and other features, pointing out how cities, mountain peaks, and mountain ranges are noted on the map. Have students work with a partner to study the physical map of the Northeast on the blackline master and write a song or poem about several of the major landforms and bodies of water. Encourage students to be specific about which features appear in which states. Have volunteers perform their songs for the class. If possible, record these performances for students to enjoy later.

··

🅴🅻🅻 Support for English Language Learners

Writing Modify the Ode to the Northeast activity as described below to provide customized instruction for all learners.

Entering: Have students take turns calling out names of landforms they could include in a poem or song. Write the words on the board. Then have students draw a picture and label the landforms they included.

Emerging: Have students draw a picture with various landforms that could be included in a poem or a song. Have students write a simple sentence to describe their drawing.

Developing: Have students share their song or poem orally as you transcribe the words. Leave blanks in the place of key words and ask students to finish the song or poem by writing in the missing words.

Expanding: Have students write their song or poem independently. Offer assistance with spelling, punctuation, and grammar revisions, then ask students to recopy the song or poem without errors.

Bridging: Have students listen to their classmates' performances and write one or two sentences from each one. If you were able to record the performances, playing the performance back would make this activity easier.

Immigrant Remembers Ellis Island

Nelly Ratner Myers was born in Vienna, Austria, in 1929. At the age of 11, she and her family immigrated to the United States. She was one of more than twelve million people who entered the United States through Ellis Island.

When she was in her sixties, she was interviewed by the National Park Service about her immigration experience. Here, she recalls seeing the Statue of Liberty for the first time.

> "When we were nearing the port I saw. I looked up. I was so thrilled to see the Statue of Liberty. I looked and I saw the sky scrapers and I was so thrilled about it because I knew something about it because my father had told me. People were jumping, they were so happy. All immigrants were so happy when we got here."

Nelly's experience at Ellis Island was not all positive, though. She came to the United States with her sister, mother, uncle, and grandmother. All but her grandmother were deaf.

> "When we left the ship and I saw so many people all over and I had to go through, what do you call it, the gate. And I had to go through the gate and they stopped us, the five of us, because there were four deaf people too much, so they had to send us to Ellis Island. They took us on the ferry to Ellis Island."

When it was discovered that four of the family members were deaf, they were held for five months at Ellis Island because officials feared the family might be a financial burden on the United States.

Eventually they were released and began their lives in New York.

When asked how her mother felt living in America, she said,

> "So happy. She loved the United States. She kissed the United States. So happy."
>
> —Nelly Ratner Myers, January 16, 1992, in an interview with Carol Bonura for the National Park Service

Famous Authors From the Northeast

The chart contains the names of some famous authors from the Northeast region. Using books from the classroom or the Library Media Center, fill in the empty columns to show the state where they lived (or are living) and one of their famous works.

Zora Neale Hurston

Author	Location	Famous Works
Zora Neale Hurston		
Nathaniel Hawthorne		
Ralph Waldo Emerson		
Stephen King		
Emily Dickinson		
Julia Alvarez		
Louisa May Alcott		

99

America's History Timeline

Work with your group to research the historical events from the founding of the United States which your teacher has assigned your group.

As you research, record important dates and brief descriptions of what happened on those dates.

When your teacher directs you, add your entries to the class timeline along with those of other groups.

Date	Event
_____	_____
_____	_____
_____	_____
_____	_____

Choose one of those entries and create an illustration of the event in the box.

Ode to the Northeast

Study this physical map of the Northeast region. On the back of this page, write a song or poem about the major landforms and bodies of water you see. Be specific about which features appear in which states.

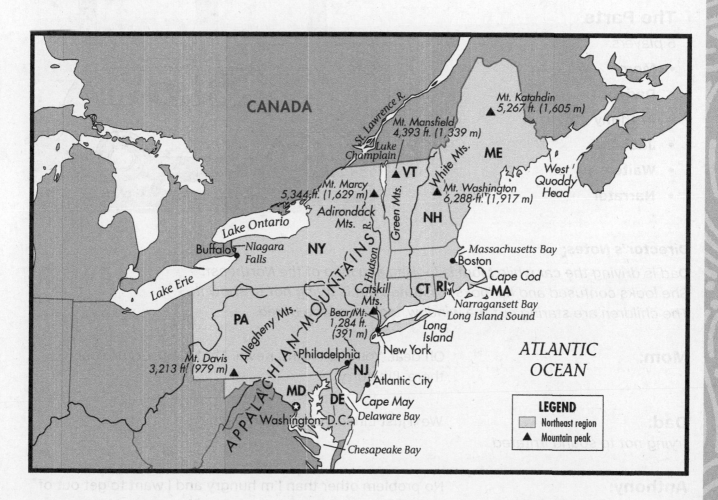

A family from Texas is enjoying a fall foliage tour driving through the Northeast region. They may or may not be slightly lost, depending on who you ask.

The Parts

6 players:

- **Mom**
- **Dad**
- **Anthony**
- **Jasmine**
- **Waiter**
- **Narrator**

Director's Notes:

Dad is driving the car while Mom is looking at a map of the Northeast.
She looks confused and he looks frustrated but is trying not to show it.
The children are staring out the window, looking a little bored.

Mom: Oh dear. You were right, Kevin. That was our turn back there. I'm sorry.

Dad: We'll just circle back. No problem.
trying not to sound irritated

Anthony: No problem other than I'm hungry and I want to get out of this car.

Dad: Anthony! I know we have been in the car all morning, but you have been impatient since New Hampshire!

Anthony: Which sounds like a much longer time than it actually has been.

Narrator: Dad continues making a series of turns as Mom points the way a little uncertainly.

Jasmine:	That's so true. I mean, we're already in Vermont. If we were in Texas, we would have to drive for hours before we would cross a state line. We have already crossed two of them today, and it isn't even lunchtime!
Anthony:	My stomach says it is.
Narrator:	Jasmine laughs.
Mom:	I wouldn't mind a little break myself. Let's pull over at this restaurant.
Narrator:	The family exits the car and enters a restaurant, where the children eat their food as Mom and Dad continue studying the map over their meals. Their server approaches to refill drinks.
Waiter:	Ah, you're here to see the fall foliage, aren't you?
Dad:	Absolutely. We're on our way home to Texas. We started in Portland, Maine, this morning. Beautiful! We got some great pictures.
Mom:	But I think we might have gotten a little off course. We wanted to cross slightly over into New York next. We're trying to visit all the states in the Northeast. I don't suppose you could help us get back on track to New York?
Waiter: *pausing, looking confused and amused*	Uh, you're more than slightly crossed over here. You're in Saratoga Springs, New York!
Everyone laughs.	
Waiter:	You should take a little hike through the North Woods at Skidmore College before you get back on the road. You won't see nicer fall foliage anywhere.
Jasmine:	Oooh! Can we, Mom? Please? I love hiking!
Mom:	Hmm, I don't know. We have to make it to our hotel in Springfield, Massachusetts, before dark.

Regions: The Northeast

Readers Theater

Waiter: Oh, you can make that easily. It's only a couple of hours from here. You have plenty of time for a hike.

Dad: I wouldn't mind stretching my legs a bit. Good suggestion. Although I don't see how the leaves could be any more impressive than what we saw this morning in Vermont and New Hampshire.

Narrator: The children and Mom nod in agreement, remembering the morning with obvious awe.

Waiter: Well, seeing fall leaves from a car is nice, but walking through a fall forest is something entirely different. Just give it a try. I don't think you'll be disappointed!

Narrator: The waiter writes down directions to the North Woods on a napkin. The parents pay for the meal, everyone says their goodbyes, and the family returns to the car. A short drive later, they arrive at their destination.

Anthony:
looking around in all directions
Wow. Just. . . . Wow!

Jasmine: I can't even think of what to say. This is like being in another world!

Dad: Surreal. The word you're looking for is surreal.

Jasmine: Sur-something, that's for sure. I didn't even know this color of yellow existed!

| Mom: | Neither did I. Stunning! |

| Dad: | Well, honey, I just have one thing to say. Thank you very, very much for getting us lost today. |

| Narrator: | The children and parents laugh, making more jokes about getting lost as they hike through the forest. After a few minutes, Anthony breaks the awed silence. |

| Anthony: | Well, I'm hungry again. Can we go now? |

| Dad: *trying to look annoyed, but looking amused instead* | You and your stomach! |

| Jasmine: | Anthony's right. Let's hit the road again, guys. There are leaves in Massachusetts waiting for us to take their picture, too. |

| Mom: | Yeah. But with my navigation skills, we'll probably end up in Pennsylvania instead! |

| Narrator: | The family laughs again as Dad points the car south toward Massachusetts. |

6 Regions: The Southeast

Objectives

- Identify where American Indian groups of the Southeast lived in the past and where they live today.
- Identify European explorers who came to the Southeast.

- Learn about the lives of African Americans in the Southeast during and after the Civil War, and during the civil rights era.
- Describe the population and industries of a present-day city in the New South.

Quest   Project-Based Learning: Spectacular Southeastern States

	Description	Duration	Materials	Participants
STEP 1 Set the Stage	Read a blackline master as an introduction to the project.	15 minutes	**Blackline Master:** Quest Kick Off	Whole Class
STEP 2 Launch the Activities	Divide students into 12 small groups.	5 minutes	**Leveled Readers:** *What's It Like in the Southeast?*; *Life in the Southeast*; *Exploring the Southeast*	Whole Class
Activity 1 American Indians of the Southeast	Research American Indians groups of the Southeast.	20 minutes	**Blackline Master:** American Indians of the Southeast, classroom or Library Media Center resources	Small Groups
Activity 2 European Exploration	Identify European explorers who came to the Southeast and research one explorer.	20 minutes	Student Activity Mat 3A Graphic Organizer, classroom or Library Media Center resources	Small Groups
Activity 3 The Civil War	Research the enslaved African population that existed in the Southeast during the Civil War era.	10 minutes	Classroom or Library Media Center resources	Small Groups
Activity 4 The Civil Rights Era **ELL**	Study a civil rights speech by John Lewis.	25 minutes	**Blackline Master:** The Civil Rights Era, classroom or Library Media Center resources	Individual
Activity 5 The New South	Determine characteristics of a present-day city in the New South.	15 minutes	Classroom or Library Media Center resources	Individual

STEP 3				
Complete the Quest Prepare Your Infographic	Complete infographic and add finishing touches.	10 minutes	Completed Quest materials	Small Groups
Present Your Infographic	Present the group's infographic to the class.	45 minutes		Small Groups
Answer the Compelling Question	Discuss the compelling question.	15 minutes		Whole Class

Quick Activities

	Description	Duration	Materials	Participants
Landforms Card Game	Play a card game about landforms in the Southeast.	20 minutes	**Blackline Master:** Landforms Card Game, index cards, art supplies	Partners
Flood Safety	Create a flood safety poster.	30 minutes	Poster board, art supplies, classroom or Library Media Center resources	Partners
World Heritage Sites	Find pictures of a World Heritage Site located in the Southeast.	30 minutes	**Blackline Master:** World Heritage Sites, classroom or Library Media Center resources, Student Activity Mat 1B United States Outline	Individual
Primary Source: George Washington Carver	Describe and analyze details in a primary source photo of George Washington Carver.	20 minutes	**Primary Source:** George Washington Carver	Individual
Read "Land of the South" ELL	Analyze a poem from the Southeast region.	20 minutes	**Blackline Master:** "Land of the South"	Individual
Readers Theater: The New South: A Center for Research	Perform a brief skit about research institutions and universities in the New South.	30 minutes	**Readers Theater:** The New South: A Center for Research	Small Groups

Project-Based Learning: Spectacular Southeastern States

Q Compelling Question How has the Southeast changed over time?

Welcome to Quest 6, Spectacular Southeastern States. In this Quest, your students will study the history of one state in the Southeast. They will use what they learn to create a colorful map-based infographic about how that state has changed over time. For each state, students will study American Indian groups, European explorers, the Civil War, the civil rights era, and the New South. They will use what they learn to create an infographic, which will prepare them to discuss the compelling question at the end of this inquiry.

Objectives

- Identify where American Indian groups of the Southeast lived in the past and where they live today.
- Identify the European explorers who came to the Southeast region.
- Learn about the lives of African Americans in the Southeast during and after the Civil War, and during the civil rights era.
- Describe the population and industries of a present-day city in the New South.

STEP 1 Set the Stage ⏱15 minutes

Begin the Quest by distributing the blackline master **Quest Kick Off.** It will bring the world of the Quest to life, introducing a story to interest students and a mission to motivate them.

Story

The governors of each state in the Southeast have requested infographics about the history of their state. The infographics will be displayed at their state capitols.

··

Mission

Students must create a colorful, map-based infographic about one of the states. The infographic will have text and images to help explain the history of the state.

STEP 2 Launch the Activities

The following five activities will help students prepare to create their infographic by guiding them through five historical topics: American Indians, European explorers, the Civil War, the civil rights era, and the New South.

Assign the appropriate Leveled Reader for this chapter.

Divide students into 12 separate small groups that will remain consistent throughout the Quest activities. Assign each group one of the following states: Virginia, West Virginia, Kentucky, Tennessee, Arkansas, Louisiana, North Carolina, South Carolina, Georgia, Mississippi, Alabama, or Florida.

Distribute a large piece of poster board to each group. The poster board should have an outline of one of these states. You may prepare this ahead of time, or make it a class activity. You may wish to label the state's capital and other major cities, or ask groups to do that.

Activity 1   **American Indians of the Southeast** 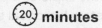 minutes

Materials: Blackline Master: American Indians of the Southeast, classroom or Library Media Center resources

Copy and distribute the blackline master **American Indians of the Southeast**. Explain that American Indian groups were here long before European explorers came to North America, and that this is true for every state.

Ask students to form their groups and find the name of the state that you have assigned them. (If their state does not have an American Indian group shown, ask students to select a neighboring state instead.) Have students study where American Indian groups of the Southeast lived in the past. Then have them use classroom or Library Media Center resources to look up their state's American Indian group (or groups) and discover where they live today. Encourage them to look on the Internet for the official Web sites of American Indian groups, and explain that the word *nation* might be used instead of *group*. For example, the official Web site of the Choctaw is www.choctawnation.com. After gathering information, have students write down their findings.

Next, have students use the Library Media Center to search for a photo or other image of one aspect of the American Indian group's culture. Examples of images might include food, housing, religion, or arts and crafts. The image could be contemporary or historical. Students should print the photo and paste it on their infographic along with a sentence that explains what it is and what group it belongs to. The photo is likely to be a "floating" image on their infographic unless groups discover a particular place in their state where the American Indian group resides, such as a reservation. (Define *reservation* for students as "an area of land set aside for use by an American Indian group.") In those cases, have them place the photo near that location and draw a leader line with a marker.

Materials: Student Activity Mat 3A Graphic Organizer, classroom or
Library Media Center resources

Explain to students that the journey to North America in 1492 led by Christopher
Columbus began an era of European exploration. Some explorers came to the
Southeast region.

Distribute Student Activity Mat 3A Graphic Organizer. Using classroom or Library
Media Center resources, have student groups find a European explorer who came
to their assigned state. Have them write the explorer's name in the top box of the
graphic organizer. Some ideas for explorers are:

- Juan Ponce de León
- Hernando de Soto
- Robert de La Salle

Students should continue their research to find where in the state the explorer
went. Have them write that information in the middle box. Finally, have them
research evidence of the explorer's presence in the state today. For example, is
there a state park or state historical site dedicated to the explorer? Or, they might
search for the influence of the explorer's cultural group or home country. Have
students add this information in the bottom box.

Students should tape their graphic organizers (or a photocopy of it) on their
infographic. If students named a specific place in their third box, have them label it
on the base map and draw a leader line from their graphic organizer to that place.

Activity 3 **The Civil War** (10) **minutes**

Materials: Classroom or Library Media Center resources

Explain that by the 1860s, about 3.5 million enslaved Africans lived in the Southeast
region. Conflicts over slavery were the main cause of a civil war that broke out in
1861 between the North, which opposed slavery, and the South, which wanted it
to remain legal. Explain that six states in the Southeast decided to form their own
country called the Confederate States of America (or the Confederacy). Eventually
other states joined the Confederacy.

Have students use classroom or Library Media Center resources to research the
following statistics:

- the population of their assigned state in 1860
- the number of enslaved Africans living in their assigned state in 1860
- the percent of the state's total population that were enslaved Africans

A good Web Site for this information is www.civil-war.net. (Navigate to "US Census
of 1860" and use the dropdown menu to identify the state.)

Have student groups create a fact chart that shows this information and paste it
on their infographics. This chart will probably be a "floating" chart.

Materials: Blackline Master: The Civil Rights Era, classroom or Library Media Center resources

Explain to students that one of the negative effects of the Civil War was widespread segregation throughout the country, and especially in the Southeast region. (Define *segregation* to students as "a system under which people of different races are kept separate.")

The fight against segregation reached a climax during the civil rights movement in the 1950s and 1960s. Many of the leaders of the civil rights movement were from the Southeast, including Rosa Parks, Martin Luther King, Jr., and John Lewis.

Distribute copies of blackline master **The Civil Rights Era** to students. Explain that in 1963, the March on Washington brought widespread attention to the civil rights issues of African Americans. The march was where Martin Luther King, Jr. gave his famous "I Have a Dream" speech, and John Lewis, a future congressman representing Georgia, also spoke. In his address, Lewis criticized the pending civil rights bill in Congress.

Have students read the excerpt silently and then answer the question: What kinds of change was John Lewis asking for? Have them write their answers on a separate piece of paper. As a group, have students choose one group member's answer to cut and paste on the infographic.

· ·

ELL **Support for English Language Learners**

Speaking Support students as they speak parts of John Lewis's speech aloud.

Entering: Speak the following from John Lewis's speech aloud in a strong, oratorical voice: "We march today for jobs and freedom." Have students imitate your delivery aloud.

Emerging: Speak the following from John Lewis's speech aloud in a strong, oratorical voice: "We march today for jobs and freedom. . . . 'One man, one vote' is the African cry. It is ours too. It must be ours!" Have students imitate your delivery aloud.

Developing: Have students work with a partner and take turns saying the following from John Lewis's speech aloud in a strong, oratorical voice: "We march today for jobs and freedom. . . . 'One man, one vote' is the African cry. It is ours too. It must be ours!"

Expanding: Have students work with a partner and take turns saying the following from John Lewis's speech aloud in a strong, oratorical voice: "We march today for jobs and freedom. . . . 'One man, one vote' is the African cry. It is ours too. It must be ours!" Have partners give positive feedback to each other and then repeat the delivery.

Bridging: Have student partners watch online footage of John Lewis giving his speech. Then have them speak aloud the entire excerpt from the blackline master, imitating Lewis's strong, oratorical voice.

Activity 5 **The New South** ⏱ **minutes**

Materials: Classroom or Library Media Center resources

Explain to students that many cities in the Southeast region have seen changes in recent years. For example, populations have increased as people moved to the region to find jobs. Also, certain industries have emerged in the region in the areas of technology and medicine. These changes have led to the region being called the New South.

Ask student groups to choose one city in their state. They should use classroom or Library Media Center resources to research the following details about the city:

- current population
- top industries there
- companies that are headquartered there
- how many jobs those companies provide

Have student groups compile this information in a chart and paste it on their infographic. They may wish to find a photo of their chosen city and paste it on their infographic as well. Both their chart and their photo should be connected with leader lines to the location of the city on the base map.

STEP 3 Complete the *Quest*

Part 1 Prepare Your Infographic ⏱ 10 minutes

Materials: Completed Quest materials

At this point, student groups should have pasted the appropriate pieces of information and images on their infographic. If they have not finished doing this, give them class time to complete these tasks. Remind them that they should draw leader lines from their pasted pieces of information to specific places on the map when appropriate.

Have students name their infographic and paste that on the top of their poster board. Encourage them to complete other finishing touches, such as:

- putting a border along the outside edge of the poster board
- coloring in areas of the map
- researching and adding labels of other cities, towns, state parks, or bodies of water

Part 2 Present Your Infographic ⏱ 45 minutes

Have groups take turns presenting their infographic. Since there will be at least five topics to present, ask groups to divide the presentation among the number of individuals. Some members will have to present more than one topic.

Part 3 Compelling Question ⏱ 15 minutes

After students complete their infographic, encourage them to reflect on what they learned. As a class, discuss the compelling question for this Quest, "How has the Southeast changed over time?"

Students have studied different periods of Southeast history. They should think about the people who have lived—and still live—in the state, and what events they have lived through. They should use what they learned to answer the compelling question.

113

Spectacular Southeastern States

The governors of the 12 states in the Southeast region need your help! They want their citizens to know more about the history of their spectacular state. Create a colorful infographic that tells ways their state has changed throughout history. Your infographic will be displayed in the state's capitol building.

Your Mission

Work in a group and create a colorful infographic about the history of one spectacular state in the Southeast. Your infographic should include information about these five historical topics: American Indians, European explorers, the Civil War, the civil rights era, and the New South.

To gather information for your infographic:

Activity 1 **American Indians of the Southeast:** Study where American Indian groups of the Southeast lived in the past and research where they live today.

Activity 2 **European Exploration:** Create a graphic organizer about European explorers who came to the Southeast.

Activity 3 **The Civil War:** Research the number of enslaved Africans who lived in the Southeast during the time of the Civil War.

Activity 4 **The Civil Rights Era:** Study a speech given by an important civil rights leader from the Southeast region.

Activity 5 **The New South:** Research top industries and current populations of a Southeast city.

Complete Your Quest

Create and present an infographic about the history of a state in the Southeast region.

Activity 1

American Indians of the Southeast

Study the map. It shows where American Indian groups lived in the Southeast region long ago. Today, members of these American Indian groups still live in the region.

Find your assigned state on the map and identify the groups that lived there long ago. Research where your state's groups live today and write down your findings.

Then, find a picture that shows one aspect of the group's culture, either today or long ago. For example, find a picture of a tool they used or a kind of home they lived in. Print the picture and paste it on your infographic with a short explanation.

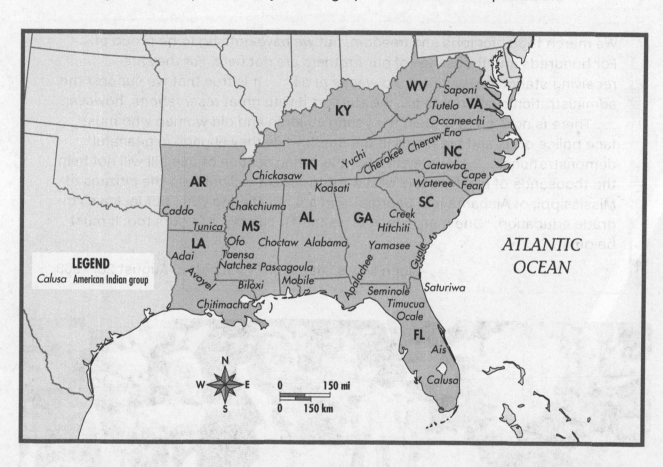

LEGEND

Calusa   American Indian group

_____

_____

_____

_____

_____

_____

The Civil Rights Era

During the 1950s and 1960s, leaders of the civil rights movement tried to end segregation between whites and African Americans. John Lewis was one of those leaders. In 1963, he gave a speech at the Lincoln Memorial in Washington, D.C., to thousands of people. In his speech, Lewis addressed a bill that would expand the civil rights of African Americans.

Read excerpts from the speech and then write your answer to this question on a separate piece of paper: What kinds of change was John Lewis asking for?

> We march today for jobs and freedom, but we have nothing to be proud of. For hundreds and thousands of our brothers are not here. For they are receiving starvation wages, or no wages at all. . . . It is true that we support the administration's civil rights bill. We support it with great reservations, however. . . . There is nothing to protect the young children and old women who must face police dogs and fire hoses in the South while they engage in peaceful demonstrations. . . . As it stands now, the voting section of this bill will not help the thousands of black people who want to vote. It will not help the citizens of ...sissippi, of Alabama and Georgia, who are qualified to vote, but lack a sixth-gr..e education. "One man, one vote" is the African cry. It is ours too. It must be ..rs!
>
> —John Lewis, March on Washington, August 28, 1963

Quick Activities

Landforms Card Game

Partners (20) **minutes**

Materials: Blackline Master: Landforms Card Game, index cards, art supplies

Put students into pairs and distribute 12 blank index cards to each student. Have them write the name of one state from the Southeast on each card. Students who are looking for an extra challenge can draw the outline of each state and not label it.

Distribute the blackline master **Landforms Card Game.** Ask student pairs to study the map. To play the game, have students shuffle their cards and divide them evenly. One student draws a card from the other student. The student says the name of a landform that is found in that state. The student may look at the map if needed. Students continue playing until both partners have drawn all the cards.

Flood Safety

Partners (30) **minutes**

Materials: Poster board, art supplies, classroom or Library Media Center resources

Explain to students that sometimes the weather in the Southeast can be dangerous. During extremely heavy rainstorms or hurricanes, rivers can flood and cause damage to people's property.

Have pairs create a flood safety poster by researching flood safety and preparation ideas. For example, this Web site from Florida is a good resource: http://www.floridadisaster.org. (Click on "Mitigation" on the left side, then click on "State Floodplain Management Office." Then scroll down below "Realtors and Property Owners," and click "Flood Preparation and Safety.")

Students' posters should offer tips and rules for how to prepare for a flood. Encourage them to mention specific bodies of water from the region. Guide a class discussion on the safety tips that most groups found.

World Heritage Sites

Individual (30) minutes

Materials: Blackline Master: World Heritage Sites, classroom or Library Media Center resources, Student Activity Mat 1B United States Outline

Distribute copies of blackline master **World Heritage Sites.** Guide students to read the list of World Heritage Sites and then pick one that interests them. Make sure that each site is selected by at least one student.

Have students use classroom or Library Media Center resources to find pictures of the place they selected. Then, they should answer the questions on the blackline master. Lead a class discussion about students' findings and opinions.

Distribute Student Activity Mat 1B United States Outline so that students can map the World Heritage Sites listed on the blackline master. Encourage students to draw a unique symbol that represents each place. For example, students may choose to draw an alligator for the Everglades National Park.

Primary Source:
George Washington Carver

Individual (20) minutes

Materials: Primary Source: George Washington Carver

Distribute copies of **Primary Source: George Washington Carver**. Ask for volunteers to read the text. Then give students silent time to study the primary source photograph of Carver in his lab and take notes on the details they see.

Then lead a class discussion in which students share their details. You may continue the discussion by asking: *How did George Washington Carver's work change the economy of the Southeast region?*

Read "Land of the South"

Materials: Blackline Master: "Land of the South"

Distribute the blackline master **"Land of the South"** and guide students as they draw arrows between the words that rhyme. Say the word *land* aloud and then ask for a volunteer to read the first stanza. Then ask students to identify a word that rhymes with *land*. Repeat this exercise for the words *rise*, *these*, *roam*, and so forth for both stanzas.

If students discover any words that are unfamiliar to them, have them use available resources to look up their definitions.

··

 Support for English Language Learners

Reading Guide students in using context clues and/or reference materials to determine the meaning of unfamiliar words.

Entering: Write the line "And green with verdure be!" on the board and say it aloud. Underline the word *verdure*. Say it aloud and ask students to repeat after you. Then circle the word *green* and draw an arrow from *green* to *verdure*. Explain that *verdure* means "greenness of fresh vegetation."

Emerging: Write the line "And green with verdure be!" on the board and say it aloud. Underline the word *verdure*. Say it aloud and ask students to repeat after you. Ask a student to come to the board and circle the word *green* and draw an arrow from *green* to *verdure*. Explain that *verdure* means "greenness of fresh vegetation."

Developing: Write the line "And green with verdure be!" on the board and say it aloud. Underline the word *verdure*. Say it aloud and ask students to repeat after you. Ask a volunteer to come to the board and circle a word that gives a context clue to the meaning of *verdure*. (green)

Expanding: Write the line "And green with verdure be!" on the board and say it aloud. Underline the word *verdure*. Say it aloud and ask students to repeat after you. Have students use a context clue from the line to decipher the meaning of the word. Then, have them explain what they did in their own words.

Bridging: Write the words *imperial*, *fair*, *roam*, and *verdure* on the board. Ask students to choose one word and explain how they would use context clues from the poem to help understand their word's meaning.

Landforms Card Game

Follow your teacher's instructions and make your own deck of Southeast playing cards. Then, with a partner, study the Southeast physical map. Draw a card from your partner. Name a landform found in the state shown on the card you drew. Then your partner will draw a card from you and name a landform in the state. Keep playing like this until you and your partner are both out of cards.

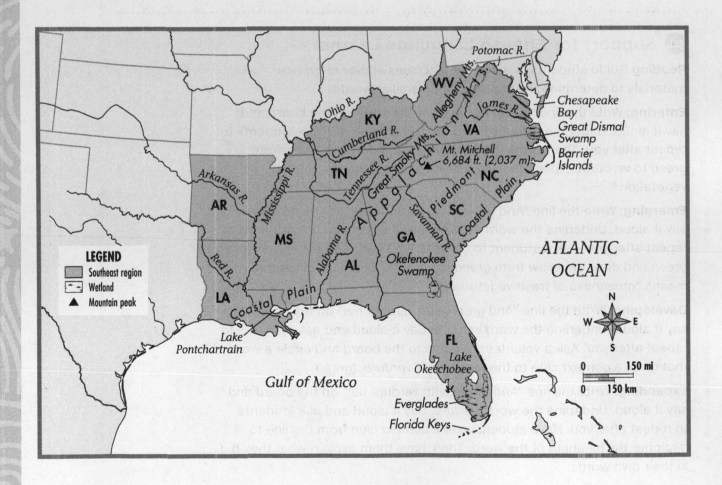

LEGEND
Southeast region
Wetland
Mountain peak

Potomac R.
WV
Ohio R.
Allegheny Mts.
James R.
Chesapeake Bay
Great Dismal Swamp
KY
Cumberland R.
VA
Barrier Islands
Mt. Mitchell 6,684 ft. (2,037 m)
TN
Tennessee R.
Great Smoky Mts.
NC
Piedmont
Coastal Plain
Arkansas R.
Appalachian
SC
AR
Savannah R.
MS
Alabama R.
GA
Mississippi R.
Red R.
AL
Okefenokee Swamp
ATLANTIC OCEAN
LA
Coastal Plain
Lake Pontchartrain
FL
Lake Okeechobee
Gulf of Mexico
Everglades
Florida Keys

N W E S

0   150 mi
0   150 km

World Heritage Sites

Read the names of the World Heritage Sites
that are located in the Southeast region.
Choose one and research images of it.
Then answer the questions.

- Everglades National Park (Florida)

- Mammoth Cave National Park (Kentucky)

- Great Smoky Mountains National Park
  (North Carolina and Tennessee)

- Monticello and the University of Virginia
  (Virginia)

- Monumental Earthworks of Poverty Point
  (Louisiana)

1. How is the World Heritage Site unique or significant?

_____

_____

_____

_____

2. Why would tourists want to visit the World Heritage Site?

_____

_____

_____

_____

Name _____ Date _____

George Washington Carver

The Southeast is a great region for farming. During the 1700s and 1800s, the region mostly grew cotton. Growing a lot of cotton damaged the soil, however.

Fun Fact
Carver also discovered more than 100 uses for sweet potatoes!

George Washington Carver was an agricultural scientist who helped the Southeast region move away from a cotton-based economy. In the 1880s, he discovered that growing peanuts and soybeans helped restore important nutrients to the soil, which made the soil healthier. Carver's work changed the economy of the Southeast forever.

Study the photograph of George Washington Carver in his laboratory. Write down all the details you notice.

_____

_____

_____

_____

_____

"Land of the South"

The poem "Land of the South" is an example of Southern literature from the 1850s. Read the poem and draw arrows between the words that rhyme. Then turn to a partner and discuss the ways in which the poem describes the Southeast. Do you think the poem successfully captures the Southeast in some way? Explain your reasoning.

"Land of the South"
by Alexander Beaufort Meek

I. LAND of the South!—imperial land!

How proud thy mountains rise!

How sweet thy scenes on every hand!

How fair thy covering skies!

But not for this—oh, not for these

I love thy fields to roam;

Thou hast a dearer spell to me,

Thou art my native home!

II. Thy rivers roll their liquid wealth,

Unequaled to the sea;

Thy hills and valleys bloom with health,

And green with verdure be!

But not for thy proud ocean streams,

Not for thy azure dome,

Sweet, sunny South, I cling to thee,

Thou art my native home!

Abby wants to study medicine in college. Maybe a university in the Southeast would be a good fit for her!

The Parts

5 players:

- **Ty De Forest**
- **Professor De Forest,** Ty's father
- **Abby Schultz**
- **Ms. Schultz,** Abby's mother
- **Narrator**

Director's Notes:

Abby and Ty are in the eleventh grade and are best friends. Ty's father is a professor at State University. He teaches biology to college students who are studying to become doctors. Biology is the study of life and all living things. Abby is very interested in being a doctor, and wonders if State University would be a good college choice. Ty is taking Abby and her mother to observe one of his father's classes.

Ty: *urgently*	C'mon, Abby, let's get a move on. We don't want to miss too much of my father's class.
Abby: *smiling*	It's so nice of your dad to let me and my mom observe him teaching. I know he's popular with his students.
Ty: *raising an eyebrow*	Yeah, but he's strict, too!
Ms. Schultz:	That's good! Biology isn't an easy subject. And it's important for future doctors to know a lot about biology.

Narrator:	Ty, Abby, and Ms. Schultz approach a lecture hall on the campus of State University. They go inside and stand at the back of the room. Professor De Forest is in the middle of his lecture. The lecture hall is full of college students. They are listening and taking notes.
Professor De Forest: *to the class*	. . . so it's very important that you learn the names of all the bones in the body—and then move on to the muscles. I expect you to have them all memorized by Monday. Now, for homework, I'd like you to read chapters 4 and 5 . . .
Ty: *whispering*	I think he's just about finished. After all the students leave, you can ask him questions about State University and his work.
Ms. Schultz: *whispering*	Does your father just teach, or does he also do research?
Ty: *whispering*	He does a lot of research. State University is one of the finest research institutions in the Southeast. You can't be a professor here and not do your own research.
Abby: *whispering*	What area of medicine does he research?
Ty: *whispering*	He works in sports medicine. He's very interested in helping athletes prevent serious injuries.
Narrator:	As the three of them whisper, Professor De Forest finishes his lecture and his students exit the lecture hall.
Professor De Forest: *gesturing to them*	Ty, bring your friends over! I've been looking forward to meeting them.
Ty:	Dad, this is my best friend, Abby, and this is Abby's mom.
Abby: *smiling and shaking his hand*	It's nice to meet you.

Ms. Schultz:
shaking his hand

Thank you for having us.

Professor De Forest:

My pleasure. Abby, Ty says you're interested in coming to State University to study medicine.

Abby:

That's right. I've always dreamed of becoming a doctor. Is the program here at State University a good one?

Professor De Forest:

It absolutely is. State University is a famous research institute for medicine, but the professors here also research technology, business, and education.

Ms. Schultz:
nodding

Abby's interested in all those subjects, but I think medicine is her real passion.

Abby:

I'm just not sure I want to live so far from home. Most of my good friends are back home in Chapel Hill.

Professor De Forest:
brightly

Chapel Hill, North Carolina? That's the home of the University of North Carolina. It's a very fine university and its School of Medicine is outstanding and well known. You could apply there.

Ty:
quizzically

Isn't UNC part of . . . what do they call that . . . the research square?

Ms. Schultz:
correcting Ty

You mean the Research Triangle.

Professor De Forest:
smiling

That's right. The Research Triangle is an area of North Carolina where there's a lot of research going on at both universities and companies. The University of North Carolina at Chapel Hill is one of many great research universities in that area.

Ty:
chiming in

Duke University is another one, I think. It's in Durham, right?

Ms. Schultz *agreeing*	Yes—and North Carolina State University is in Raleigh. That's the other big school.
Abby: *excitedly*	Those all sound like great options!
Professor De Forest:	They are. There are many colleges and universities in other parts of the Southeast, too. Have you ever heard the Southeast referred to as the "New South"? The New South refers to all the economic changes that have been going on in the Southeast for many years.
Ms. Schultz: *nodding her head*	That's right. Long ago, the South's economy was based on agriculture and most people lived in the country. Then the economy became more industrial, and people moved to cities.
Professor De Forest: *agreeing*	And, recently, the economy became more service based. People found jobs in service industries like health care, communications, technology, tourism, and banking.
Ty:	I guess a lot of people come to the Southeast to study at one of its universities, and then they find jobs, right?
Ms. Schultz:	Exactly. People work in those service industries, or in research and education, like Professor De Forest here.
Professor De Forest: *looking at the clock*	Gang, I have to run. I'm teaching another class in an hour, and I have to meet some students first. Abby, it was great to meet you. I hope I've given you some helpful information about studying here at State University.
Abby:	You sure have, and I also know that there are other great research institutions in the Southeast that I could attend. Those universities in North Carolina's Research Triangle sound especially good—I could even live at home.
Ms. Schultz: *delighted*	Your dad and I would love that! We'll see!

Chapter 7

Regions: The Midwest

Objectives

- Identify the 12 states that make up the Midwest region.
- Name important cities in the Midwest and the reasons they are important.
- Describe historical and cultural places in the Midwest.
- Learn about the Northwest Ordinance.
- Research foods that are produced in the Midwest.

Quest Document-Based Writing: Midwest Vacation				
	Description	**Duration**	**Materials**	**Participants**
STEP 1 Set the Stage	Read a blackline master and an introduction to the project.	15 minutes	**Blackline Master:** Quest Kick Off	Whole Class
STEP 2 Launch the Activities	Discuss upcoming activities and background information.	5 minutes	**Video:** "Nebraska: Great Land for Farming"	Whole Class
Activity 1 Midwest Geography	Label the states and important cities of the Midwest region on a map.	20 minutes	**Blackline Master:** Midwest Geography, **Leveled Readers:** *What's It Like in the Midwest?; Life in the Midwest; Exploring the Midwest,* Student Activity Mat 1A United States	Individual
Activity 2 Midwest Waterways	Label the lakes and rivers of the Midwest region.	20 minutes	Completed Quest materials from Activity 1	Individual
Activity 3 Midwest Cities	Research one of the biggest or most important cities in the Midwest.	30 minutes	**Blackline Master:** Midwest Cities, Web graphic organizer	Partners
Activity 4 Midwest History	Research a place of historical significance in the Midwest.	30 minutes	**Blackline Master:** Midwest History, Web graphic organizer	Partners
Activity 5 Midwest Culture	Research an entertainment, art, or cultural site in the Midwest.	30 minutes	**Blackline Master:** Midwest Culture, Web graphic organizer	Partners
STEP 3 ELL Complete the Quest Write a Persuasive Letter	Write a letter describing a place in the Midwest region worthy of visiting.	30 minutes	**Blackline Master:** Write Your Letter, completed Web graphic organizer	Individual
Answer the Compelling **Question**	Discuss the compelling question.	5 minutes		Whole Class

Quick Activities

	Description	Duration	Materials	Participants
Inside a Tornado ELL	Read about one woman's experience during a tornado.	30 minutes	**Blackline Master:** Inside a Tornado	Individual
Midwest Meal Plan	Create a menu using only foods grown in the Midwest region.	20 minutes	**Blackline Master:** Midwest Meal Plan, Student Activity Mat 1B United States Outline	Small Groups, Individual
What If?	Study the Northwest Ordinance and Imagine the United States without it.	20 minutes	**Primary Source:** What If?	Individual
Midwest Matching	Create and play a matching game about the Midwest region.	20 minutes	Index cards, writing instruments	Partners
Readers Theater: Cahokia Conversation	Perform a brief skit about a group of friends discussing their field trip to Cahokia Mounds.	20 minutes	**Readers Theater:** Cahokia Conversation	Small Groups

Document-Based Writing: Midwest Vacation

Compelling Question ## What makes a place interesting to visit?

Welcome to Quest 7, Midwest Vacation. In this Quest, students will research the geography, history, and culture of the Midwest. They will use what they learn to write a persuasive letter about the Midwest, which will prepare them to discuss the compelling question at the end of this inquiry.

Objectives

- Identify the 12 states that make up the Midwest region.
- Name important cities in the Midwest and the reasons they are important.
- Describe historical and cultural places in the Midwest.

STEP 1 Set the Stage ⏱ 15 minutes

Begin the Quest by distributing the blackline master **Quest Kick Off.** It will bring the world of the Quest to life, introducing a story to interest students and a mission to motivate them.

Story

Tell students that their parents have announced that the next family vacation will be to the Midwest region, but they are unsure where exactly in the region to visit.

Mission

Students must research various aspects of the Midwest in order to make a recommendation to their parents about where in the region the family should spend their vacation.

STEP 2   Launch the Activities

The following five activities will help students prepare for their letter writing by building their knowledge of the area. Note that all five can be done independently of the larger Quest.

Begin by showing the chapter video "Nebraska: Great Land for Farming," which will give students the content background they need to complete the activities.

Then divide students into partner groups that will remain consistent for all the activities.

Activity 1   Midwest Geography   minutes

Materials: Blackline Master: Midwest Geography, Leveled
Readers: *What's It Like in the Midwest?*, *Life in the Midwest, Exploring the Midwest,* Student Activity Mat 1A United States

Use Student Activity Mat 1A United States (both political and physical maps) to identify the states that comprise the Midwest. Tell students that the Midwest is the area between the Rocky Mountains and the Appalachian Mountains. Ask students to use the information on the two maps to guess which states make up the Midwest. Students may be tempted to name southern states between the mountain ranges as well, but remind them that there are other regions in the United States—namely the Southeast and the Southwest.

Eventually students should arrive at the conclusion that the Midwest is really the 12 northernmost states between the Rockies and the Appalachians.

Distribute the blackline master **Midwest Geography**, which students will use to identify the states and major cities that make up the Midwest region.

Encourage students to use Student Activity Mat 1A United States to label each state and an important city on the blackline master. Also discuss the geographic features of the area before closing.

This is a good place for students to explore the Leveled Readers, though they could be moved to any of the Quest activities if needed. Assign the appropriate Leveled Readers to students: *What's It Like in the Midwest?*, *Life in the Midwest, Exploring the Midwest.*

Activity 2 Midwest Waterways ⏱ 20 minutes

Materials: Completed Quest materials from Activity 1

Tell students that water is very important to the Midwest region. In addition to the four Great Lakes, the longest river in the United States (the Missouri River) and the river that carries the most water (the Mississippi River) are both here, meeting just north of St. Louis. Jones-Confluence Point State Park is there, where they can stand with one river on each side of them. The rivers are different colors, so they can actually see the waters mingling. This park also features some Lewis and Clark history, since this is where their journey west to the Pacific Ocean began. (You can share pictures of the confluence with the class by visiting: mostateparks.com and searching Edward "Ted" and Pat Jones-Confluence Point State Park.)

Also spend time detailing each of the four Great Lakes that touch the Midwest, explaining that some people think of these as inland oceans, since standing on the shores of them can feel like looking across an ocean due to their vast size.

Ask students to brainstorm what kinds of recreational activities might take place on these waterways (bird-watching, boating, swimming, fishing, ice fishing, sailing, river cruises).

With the help of Student Activity Mat 1A United States, have students label each of the rivers and lakes discussed using the completed **Midwest Geography** blackline master from Activity 1.

Activity 3 Midwest Cities ⏱ 30 minutes

Materials: Blackline Master: Midwest Cities, Web graphic organizer

Have students work in pairs to conduct quick research online regarding one of the biggest or most important cities in the Midwest. Tell students to use the blackline master **Midwest Cities** prompts as their guide. Some cities from which students may choose include:

- Chicago
- Columbus
- Detroit
- Indianapolis
- Milwaukee
- Minneapolis
- St. Louis

Have pairs share their one or two most important findings about their city with the entire class.

Distribute the Web graphic organizer where listeners can take notes on each city. The graphic organizer will be used in the remaining activities.

Activity 4   Midwest History   (30) minutes

Materials: Blackline Master: Midwest History, Web graphic organizer

With the same partners as before, have students research a historical site in the Midwest. Some suggestions are:

- Mount Rushmore/the Badlands
- Cherokee Trail of Tears
- Route 66
- Cahokia Mounds
- Moline, Illinois (birthplace of John Deere tractors)

Ask students to use the blackline master **Midwest History** to guide their research.

As before, have pairs share one to two fascinating details about the historical place they researched. However, have all pairs who studied that area present at the same time so that listeners can work in just one area of their Web graphic organizer. After all pairs have presented, listeners should have a brief overview of the place that they can reference as they complete the Quest.

Activity 5   Midwest Culture   (30) minutes

Materials: Blackline Master: Midwest Culture, Web graphic organizer

With the same partners as before, have students research an entertainment, art, or cultural attraction in the Midwest. Some suggestions are:

- Rock and Roll Hall of Fame (Cleveland)
- Guthrie Theater (Minneapolis)
- Branson, Missouri
- The Field Museum (Chicago)
- The Art Institute of Chicago
- Nelson-Atkinson Museum (Kansas City)
- Madison County, Iowa, covered bridges
- Door County, Wisconsin
- Carhenge (Alliance, Nebraska)

Ask students to use the blackline master **Midwest Culture** to guide their research.

As before, have pairs share one to two fascinating details about the cultural attraction they researched. However, have all pairs who studied that attraction present at the same time so that listeners can work in just one area of their Web graphic organizer. After all pairs have presented, listeners should have a brief overview of the attraction that they can reference as they complete the Quest.

STEP 3 Complete the *Quest*

Part 1 Write a Persuasive Letter (30) minutes

Materials: Blackline Master: Write Your Letter, completed Web graphic organizer

Have students meet with their partners to review the notes they took during the Quest Activities, referring to the blackline masters they completed during research and the graphic organizer they filled out while listening to other students present their findings. From this information, students should select one place in the Midwest they might like to visit. Using the blackline master **Write Your Letter** have students write a persuasive letter to their parents describing why this area would be a good place for their family to visit.

Use the Opinion Writing rubric to assess students' letters.

🄔 Support for English Language Learners

Writing Guide students to practice their writing skills as they complete the Quest.

Entering: Have students dictate their letters instead of writing them. Then, review written letters with students and have them practice writing one sentence.

Emerging: Have students dictate their letters. As an adult transcribes the letter, leave blanks in the place of certain key words. Ask students to fill in those key words to complete the letter.

Developing: Have students dictate their letter. After the letter is transcribed, ask students to use the transcribed letter to rewrite it themselves.

Expanding: Have students write their letters independently. When they have finished, ask them to trade letters with another student and edit each other's writing.

Bridging: After students write their letters independently, ask them to work with a partner to revise and later edit the writing. Remind them that *revising* pertains to the content of the letter, while *editing* refers to grammar and spelling. Encourage students to look for ways to make each other's writing more compelling, such as adding interesting details or vivid descriptions.

Part 2 Answer the Compelling Question (5) minutes

After students write their persuasive letters, encourage them to reflect on what they learned. As a class, discuss the compelling question for this Quest, "What makes a place interesting to visit?"

Describe what students have learned and what they should think about. Remind students that they have learned about the geography, history, and culture of the Midwest in this Quest. They should use what they learned to answer the compelling question.

Midwest Vacation

Your parents have announced this year's family vacation will be to the Midwest. However, they can't decide which of the many places to visit and what to do while there. They have asked for your help choosing.

> **Your Mission**
> Write a letter to your parents describing a place in the Midwest you would like to visit.

To write your letter:

Activity 1   **Midwest Geography:** Label a map with the 12 states and important cities of the Midwest region.

Activity 2   **Midwest Waterways:** Label a map with the rivers and lakes that are found in the Midwest.

Activity 3   **Midwest Cities:** Research important cities in the Midwest.

Activity 4   **Midwest History:** Research important historical places in the Midwest.

Activity 5   **Midwest Culture:** Research important cultural places in the Midwest.

Complete Your Quest

Write a letter to your parents describing the place in the Midwest you would like to visit.

Name _____ Date _____

Midwest Geography

Label each state and important cities on the map of the Midwest region.

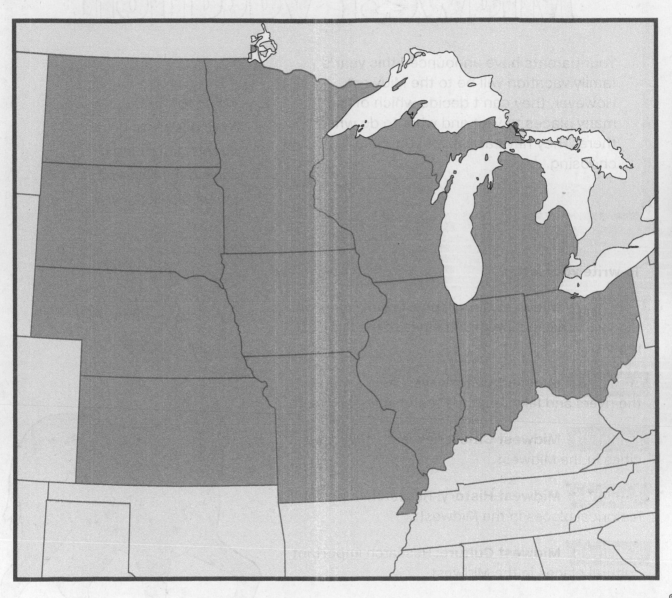

Activity 3

Name _____ Date _____

Midwest Cities

Work with a partner to research a city in the Midwest.

- Chicago
- Milwaukee
- Columbus
- Minneapolis
- Detroit
- St. Louis
- Indianapolis

St. Louis Arch

Record the details about your city.

What this city is most known for:

_____

_____

Museums in this city:

_____

_____

Entertainment/cultural attractions in this city:

_____

_____

Interesting monuments and landmarks in this city:

_____

_____

Historical events that occurred in this city:

_____

_____

Other notable things about this city:

_____

_____

Name _____ Date _____

Midwest History

Work with a partner to research a historical area in the Midwest.

- Mount Rushmore/the Badlands
- Cherokee Trail of Tears
- Route 66
- Cahokia Mounds
- Moline, Illinois (birthplace of John Deere tractors)

Record the details about your area.

Mount Rushmore

Why this place is important:

_____

_____

_____

Interesting things to see here:

_____

_____

_____

Fascinating facts about this area:

_____

_____

_____

Things we want to know more about:

_____

_____

_____

Activity 5

Name _____ Date _____

Midwest Culture

Work with a partner to research an entertainment, arts, or cultural attraction in the Midwest.

- Rock and Roll Hall of Fame (Cleveland)
- Guthrie Theater (Minneapolis)
- Branson, Missouri
- The Field Museum (Chicago)
- The Art Institute of Chicago
- Nelson-Atkinson Museum (Kansas City)
- Madison County, Iowa, covered bridges
- Door County, Wisconsin
- Carhenge (Alliance, Nebraska)

Carhenge

Record the details about your attraction.

What this attraction is famous for:

_____

_____

_____

Interesting things to see here:

_____

_____

_____

Fascinating facts about this attraction:

_____

_____

_____

Things we want to know more about:

_____

_____

_____

Write Your Letter

Meet with your partner to review the notes you took during these activities. Choose one location you would like to learn more about. On your own, finish researching the area.

When you are finished, write a persuasive letter telling your parents your opinion about visiting this place.

_____ (Date)

_____
(Greeting)

_____

_____

_____

_____

_____

_____

_____

_____
(Closing)

_____
(Signature)

Inside a Tornado

Materials: Blackline Master: Inside a Tornado

Distribute the blackline master **Inside a Tornado.** Read the story of Sandy Latimer to students. She took shelter from the 2011 Joplin, Missouri, tornado in a convenience store walk-in cooler with several strangers. Although the building around them was destroyed, they managed to escape serious injury.

Use the article and the questions that follow it to review the main idea and details as well as summarizing. The final two questions can serve as a good introduction to mood, tone, and the importance of word choice.

⬤ Support for English Language Learners

Reading Support students as they practice their reading and decoding skills.

Entering: Read the article aloud to students. Have them highlight key vocabulary words as you read them. Support students as they take turns reading parts of the article aloud.

Emerging: Read the article aloud one paragraph at a time as students follow along. Paraphrase or summarize each paragraph for students after reading it. Pair students and have them read the article aloud to each other. Ask students to answer the summarizing question aloud.

Developing: Read the article aloud to students, one or two sentences at a time. At each pause, ask students to point out words or phrases they do not understand. Provide definitions or examples to clarify meaning. Then, have pairs of students take turns reading the sentences aloud to each other.

Expanding: Have students read the article to themselves, highlighting unfamiliar words or unclear phrases. Then, have them take turns reading the article aloud with a partner. Offer definitions and substitute phrases to clarify meaning.

Bridging: Have students read the article to themselves unassisted. Encourage them to use context clues to try to determine the meaning of unknown words or phrases. If they are unable to find the meaning from context, have students consult a dictionary.

Midwest Meal Plan

Small Groups, Individual (20) minutes

Materials: Blackline Master: Midwest Meal Plan, Student Activity Mat 1B
United States Outline

Have students work in groups of four to research top foods produced in each of the Midwest region states. Since there are 12 states, each student should locate information for three states.

When students have found all the information they were assigned, have group members share their information so that all students can add at least one product to every state on Student Activity Mat 1B United States Outline.

Distribute the blackline master **Midwest Meal Plan**. Have them fill in the menu with a breakfast, lunch, or dinner plan that could be created using only products from the Midwest. Ask volunteers to share their menu.

You could even host one of these meals in the class!

What If?

Materials: Primary Source: What If?

Tell students that the Northwest Territory was created from an act passed by Congress called the Northwest Ordinance. On a classroom map, outline Ohio, Illinois, Indiana, Wisconsin, and Michigan, along with a sliver of northwest Minnesota. Tell students this was the area known as the Northwest Territory. You may wish to read other excerpts from the ordinance aloud or show a copy of it (available at ourdocuments.gov).

Tell students that the document calls for the Northwest Territory to be organized into "not less than three nor more than five" states. Using the classroom map, ask students to imagine how the states might have been created differently. For example, how might the area have been divided into three states? Which states might not exist? What might the three states have been called?

Then distribute **Primary Source: What If?** as you explain that the Northwest Ordinance contained other guidelines as well. Have students read the excerpts containing some of these and then answer the questions. If students need help with the final question, point out that the Northwest Ordinance was used as a model for creating other states as the United States expanded west. Ask them to imagine how the rest of the country might have developed differently if the Northwest Ordinance had not contained the excerpts. Ask a few volunteers to share their responses aloud.

Midwest Matching

Materials: index cards, writing instruments

Have pairs of students create a matching game. They should write the name of a state on one card and a fact or detail they have learned about that state on the other card.

After they have created the cards, have them spread out the cards facedown on a desk. As players turn over two cards at a time, they attempt to match the state with the fact. The winning player is the one who collects the most matches.

If desired, have pairs repeat the activity with another group's cards.

Inside a Tornado

Read this excerpt from a magazine article about a woman who lived through one of the deadliest tornadoes in United States history. The 2011 tornado in Joplin, Missouri, was rated EF-5, which is the strongest rating a tornado can receive.

Sandy Latimer has always been unusually terrified of thunderstorms. And not big ones, either. Just a little rain, a little lightning, a few claps and rumbles in the middle of the night, and she'll tumble out of bed and head straight to her living room and sit in the middle of it, on her carpet, which she realizes is probably no safer than staying in bed, but still feels safer for some reason. She's fifty-four years old, and this phobia has followed her around her entire life. Her mom thinks it may have been passed down to her like a virus, from a storm-phobic older cousin she played with a lot as a toddler, but to Sandy the fear seems like something innate, something integral to her being.

So the terror she experienced even before she pulled into the Fastrip, even before the lights went out, even before she huddled in the back with all the others, was raw and potent.

Then Sandy felt the wall behind her begin to move, in and out, as though it were breathing, as though she had taken shelter against the chest of some enormous creature and the creature was now waking up. The sensation kicked her terror up to another level.

When the windows explode, Sandy's mind is already incandescent with panic.

She can't make a sound, and when she tries to stand up, she finds she can't do that, either, but instead falls to the ground. She tries to crawl toward the opening, toward the door of the cooler that someone has just yanked open, the opening that all these people are now rushing toward. It's not working. It's like her body has abandoned her. It's like it won't do what she wants it to do, like the air, now full of flying glass, has become soupy, heavy, quicksandish, like the air in a nightmare.

1. Circle the main idea of the first paragraph.

2. Underline two details that support the main idea of the first paragraph.

3. How would you summarize this article in just one or two sentences?

_____

_____

_____

4. What feeling does the author try to make readers experience?

_____

5. What words or phrases does the author use to bring this feeling to readers?

_____

Midwest Meal Plan

Work with a group of three other students to research foods that are produced in each state in the Midwest region. Work together to draw these products on Student Activity Mat 1B United States Outline in the Midwest state they are produced.

Then use this information to write a menu for a meal of your choice using only products from the Midwest.

Name _____ Date _____

What If?

The Northwest Ordinance was an act passed by Congress that created the Northwest Territory, which would eventually become Wisconsin, Michigan, Illinois, Indiana, Ohio, and a small portion of Minnesota. In addition to defining the boundaries of the territory, the ordinance also laid out other important guidelines.

Read the excerpts from the Northwest Ordinance of 1787.

> Religion, morality, and knowledge being necessary to good government and the happiness of mankind, schools and the means of education shall forever be encouraged. The utmost good faith shall always be observed toward the Indians . . .
>
> There shall be neither slavery nor involuntary servitude in the said territory, otherwise than in the punishment of crimes, whereof the party shall have been duly convicted . . .

1. What are the two main guidelines the first excerpt establishes?

   _____

   _____

   _____

2. What position does the second excerpt of the ordinance take toward slavery?

   _____

   _____

3. How might the United States have been different if the ordinance had only defined the boundaries of the Northwest Territory?

   _____

   _____

Cahokia Mounds is an archeological site located near present-day St. Louis on the Mississippi River. Cahokia was an important trading center thousands of years ago, with people coming from hundreds of miles away to exchange goods. Cahokia's rich soil and flat land made it the perfect place to grow large quantities of corn, which residents traded for other items like copper, shells, tools, and more.

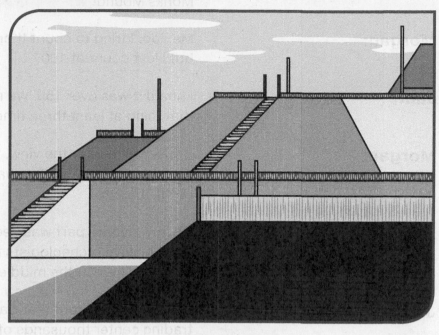

Ancient people constructed more than 100 mounds in the area, each with its own purpose. Some were burial mounds. Others were used to mark borders. The flat-topped mounds were sites of important buildings. About 70 mounds have been preserved at Cahokia.

Over the years, archeologists have discovered many artifacts and structures that have provided information about how the Mississippian culture lived thousands of years ago, but little is known for sure about why Cahokia was abandoned around the thirteenth century.

As four classmates are returning from their field trip to Cahokia Mounds, they are discussing the things they learned and debating some of the mysteries about what led to Cahokia's downfall.

The Parts

4 players:

- **Jarrett**, a fourth-grade boy
- **Morgan**, a fourth-grade girl
- **Juan**, a fourth-grade boy
- **Aisha**, a fourth-grade girl

Director's Notes:

Jarrett, Morgan, Juan, and Aisha are seated near each other on a school bus as their fourth-grade class returns from a trip to Cahokia Mounds. The students are talking excitedly about their day.

Jarrett:	Ouch! My legs are sore from walking all those steps up Monks Mound!
Morgan:	Me, too. I tried to count them on the way back down, but I lost count at 100.
Juan:	I heard it was over 150. We must have gone up and down that thing at least three times.
Morgan: *with excitement*	It was worth it for the view, though. That was my favorite part. I could see the Gateway Arch so clearly from the top of the mound.
Aisha:	Oh, my favorite part was seeing the artifacts. I still can't believe archeologists have found shark teeth and seashells here in the middle of the country!
Juan:	I guess that is proof that Cahokia was an important trading center thousands of years ago. The people here must have traded corn and tools they made for exotic items like shells and shark teeth. If it was so important and so many people lived here though, I wonder why it was abandoned.
Jarrett:	I agree with the guide who said it was probably a war. The whole area was surrounded by a giant wall with guard towers and places for archers. Obviously someone was threatening the residents.
Morgan: *shaking her head doubtfully*	I don't know. I think they were able to defend themselves from enemies just fine thanks to that wall. Did you see all the arrowheads on display? The Mississippians made a lot of weapons! It could have been a civil war perhaps, but I think it might have been the effect of such a big population on the area.
Aisha:	I agree, Morgan. Think about it: they said over 20,000 people lived there at one point. If the corn crop failed one year, the people could have easily starved.
Juan:	Yes, but they still would have had all the animals and fish in the area. I don't think they starved because of a bad crop.

Jarrett:	Without a corn crop, people probably would have stopped coming to trade with the locals, though. Cahokia might have lost its popularity after a crop failure or two.
Morgan: *nodding*	True. Maybe since the Mississippi River is so close, there could have been a great flood that wiped out the corn one year. Or if some of the traders brought a disease with them, so many people in such a small area could have quickly died of illness.
Jarrett:	Right, or they could have run out of resources in this area. Trying to support the villagers plus all the people who came to trade couldn't have been easy. Remember that at one point it had a larger population than London!
Juan:	Maybe they ran out of animals to hunt, or trees to use for building homes and other structures. The guide said it took over 15,000 logs to build the wall around the city, right?
Morgan:	Yes, and archeologists think they built that wall three times. That's a lot of trees to cut down!
Aisha: *looking confused*	Hmmm. Too many possibilities and too little information.
Jarrett:	I still think it was a war, though.
Juan:	I guess we'll never know.
Aisha:	Don't be so sure! Archeologists still have a lot more of the area to study. I think we'll find out someday!
Juan:	Hey, I think I just figured out what I want to be when I grow up!
Morgan: *rubbing her sore legs*	What an interesting job! We could be a team solving the mysteries of Cahokia, except I don't think I have strong enough legs to climb up, down, and around those 70 mounds all day.

The children laugh.

8 Regions: The Southwest

Objectives

- Analyze the importance of water conservation in the Southwest region.
- Map weather patterns and average temperatures in four cities of the Southwest.
- Investigate the top industries of the Southwest and hold a mock interview.
- Identify and promote popular tourist attractions in the Southwest region.

Quest Project-Based Learning: From the News Desk

	Description	Duration	Materials	Participants
STEP 1 Set the Stage	Read a blackline master as an introduction to the project.	5 minutes	**Blackline Master:** Quest Kick Off	Whole Class
STEP 2 Launch the Activities	Watch a video with background information.	5 minutes	**Video:** "Arizona: A Sunny Wonderland" **Leveled Readers:** *What's It Like in the Southwest?*, *Life in the Southwest*, *Exploring the Southwest*	Whole Class
Activity 1 Our Environment Today and Tomorrow	Research the importance of water conservation in the Southwest and identify ten water conservation tips.	20 minutes	Classroom or Library Media Center resources	Small Groups
Activity 2 Weather Report	Conduct research to learn about weather patterns and climate in four cities of the Southwest.	30 minutes	**Blackline Master:** Weather Report, classroom or Library Media Center resources	Small Groups
Activity 3 The Southwest Works	Investigate the top industries of the Southwest and hold a mock interview with someone from this industry.	40 minutes	Classroom or Library Media Center resources	Small Groups
Activity 4 Commercial Break	Research a tourist attraction in the Southwest region and create a 60-second commercial.	30 minutes	Student Activity Mat 3A Graphic Organizer, classroom or Library Media Center resources	Small Groups

STEP 3 Complete the Quest Prepare the Newscast	Use research notes to prepare and rehearse the newscast.	(40) minutes	Completed Quest materials	Small Groups
Deliver a **ELL** Presentation	Students present a newscast.	(30) minutes		Small Groups
Answer the **Compelling Question**	Discuss the compelling question.	(10) minutes		Whole Class
Quest Reflection	Reflect on the Quest.	(5) minutes	Student Activity Mat 4B Quest	Individuals

Quick Activities

	Description	Duration	Materials	Participants
We Were Ready! **ELL**	Research and write a letter explaining disaster safety.	(20) minutes	Classroom or Library Media Center resources	Individuals
Hopi Farming	Learn about the farming techniques used by the Hopi.	(20) minutes	**Blackline Master:** Hopi Farming	Partners
Primary Source: The Grand Canyon	Read a primary source journal entry before writing a description of the Grand Canyon.	(20) minutes	**Primary Source:** The Grand Canyon, highlighters, Student Activity Mat 3B Time and Place	Individuals
Flags and Mottos	Match state flags and state mottos to the Southwest states.	(15) minutes	**Blackline Master:** Flags and Mottos, scissors, glue	Small Groups
Readers Theater: The Alamo	Perform a brief skit about the Battle of the Alamo.	(20) minutes	**Readers Theater:** The Alamo	Small Groups

Project-Based Learning: From the News Desk

What forms the character of a region?

Welcome to Quest 8, From the News Desk. In this Quest, students will investigate the factors that contribute to the character of a region, and in particular, the Southwest. They will analyze environmental factors, such as climate and weather patterns, as well as social factors, such as industries and tourist attractions. After participating in the Quest activities, students will be prepared to discuss the compelling question at the end of this inquiry.

Objectives

- Analyze the importance of water conservation in the Southwest region.
- Map weather patterns and average temperatures in four cities of the Southwest.
- Investigate the top industries of the Southwest and hold a mock interview.
- Identify and promote popular tourist attractions in the Southwest region.

STEP 1 Set the Stage ⑤ minutes

Begin the Quest by distributing the blackline master **Quest Kick Off.** It will bring the world of the Quest to life, introducing a story to interest students and a mission to motivate them.

Story

The crew of an Amarillo television news station has called out sick. Students are asked to develop a newscast, complete with separate segments, to fill in for the sick crew.

....

Mission

Students will examine the characteristics of the Southwest region by researching, creating, and presenting their news segments.

The following four activities will help students prepare for their newscast by leading them through investigations of specific characteristics of a region. Note that all four can be done independently of the larger Quest.

Begin by showing the chapter video "Arizona: A Sunny Wonderland," which will give students the content background they need to complete the activities. You may also assign the appropriate Leveled Reader for this chapter.

Then divide students into small groups that will remain consistent for all the activities.

Activity 1 **Our Environment Today and Tomorrow** minutes

Materials: Classroom or Library Media Center resources

Explain to students that they will conduct research to be used in the environmental segment of the newscast "Our Environment Today and Tomorrow." Tell students that the focus of this news segment is water conservation in the Southwest.

In their groups, have students conduct research using classroom or Library Media Center resources on the topic.

Instruct students to identify reasons and supporting evidence for water conservation. Then, have students identify the ten most helpful water conservation tips they can share with the viewers of the newscast. Instruct students to write these tips in a "Top Ten List" for the newscast.

Activity 2 **Weather Report** minutes

Materials: Blackline Master: Weather Report, classroom or Library Media Center resources

Tell groups that they will be conducting research to prepare for a weather report during the newscast. Instruct groups to search for typical weather patterns and average temperatures of the Southwest. Although the news station is located in Amarillo, remind students that many viewers from the Southwest region will be watching. Encourage students to identify four cities to include in their weather report that are good representations of the Southwest's climate.

Distribute the blackline master, **Weather Report,** which includes a blank map of the Southwest region that students will use to record and visually present weather information. Remind students to label the four cities. Encourage them to draw and color weather symbols or temperature symbols on the map.

Materials: Classroom or Library Media Center resources

Explain that students will imagine they are planning a live remote television interview with someone who works in one of the top industries of the Southwest.

During this segment, the reporter will visit the guest at his or her job to do a live report. Explain that the guest should give viewers an overview of the history of the industry. Remind students that during live interviews, reporters must be prepared with both questions and answers so that they can step in and help if the guest becomes uncomfortable in front of the camera or needs help making a point. Live broadcasts have only a few minutes to devote to each segment, so reporters must be sure they are prepared to keep guests on topic.

Instruct groups to use classroom or Library Media resources to do research on one of the top industries of the Southwest:

- Oil

- Tourism

- Cattle/Ranching

- Solar/Alternative Energy

Have students create fictional interview questions, such as:

- How long have you been working in your industry?

- What are some benefits of working in your industry?

- What are some challenges?

- How might your industry change in the next ten years?

Once groups have researched sufficient information on the industry, have students work on the interview outline and practice the mock interview.

156

Activity 4 **Commercial Break** (30) minutes

Materials: Student Activity Mat 3A Graphic Organizer, classroom or
Library Media Center resources

Explain to students that local news broadcast stations often provide advertising
slots to local or regional attractions. Assign each group a type of tourist attraction
(such as theme park, zoo, national park, or museum) found in the Southwest. Then
have groups use classroom or Library Media Center resources to conduct online
research about the attraction and develop a 60-second commercial script to air
during the broadcast.

Instruct students to use Student Activity Mat 3A Graphic Organizer to organize the
information they collect during their research. Have students label the first section
of the mat "Location—City and State," the second section "Operating Days and
Hours," and the third section "Fun and Interesting Things to Do." Have students
use the information recorded on Student Activity Mat 3A Graphic Organizer to help
them prepare their 60-second commercial.

STEP 3 Complete the *Quest*

Part 1 **Prepare the Newscast** (40) minutes

Materials: Completed Quest materials

Have groups work together to prepare notes for the broadcast. Instruct students
to assign each member of the small group to serve as one member of the news
team (news anchor, weather reporter, live remote reporter, interviewee, commercial
advertiser). Explain to students that they must work together to bridge these
separate segments into a complete news program. Tell students to consider
and make notes about how they will transition from one segment of the news
broadcast to the next.

Provide students ample time to practice and rehearse their news broadcast.
Remind students that the more they practice, the smoother the transitions will be
between segments.

Part 2 **Deliver a Presentation** (30) minutes

Allow student groups to perform their broadcast. Depending on time constraints
and resources, the broadcast may be conducted live in front of the class, or may
be recorded using video equipment and viewed at a later time.

Support for English Language Learners

Speaking Explain to students that speaking clearly helps listeners (or viewers) to better understand the ideas that are being presented.

Entering: Prior to presenting the news report, allow each student time to practice one-on-one with you. For example, point to the name of a tourist attraction to be presented in the commercial and say the name aloud. Have the student repeat the name after you. Then have the student use body language along with a simple word to show excitement about the attraction, such as saying, "Fun!" while smiling and jumping into the air. Continue practicing until the student is confident enough to present the segment to a small group.

Emerging: Prior to presenting the news report, allow each student time to practice one-on-one with you. For example, point to the name of a tourist attraction to be presented in the commercial and say a sentence about the attraction aloud, such as "The zoo is fun for families." Have the student repeat the sentence after you. Then have the student use body language along with the sentence to show excitement about the attraction. Continue practicing until the student is confident

Developing: Prior to presenting the news report, allow each student time to practice with a partner. Have the partners practice saying at least three sentences relating to their chosen segments. Have partners continue to practice by saying the three sentences aloud until they are confident enough to present the segment to a small group.

Expanding: Prior to presenting the news report, allow each student time to practice with a small group. Have the student practice saying three to five sentences related to the segment, and have the group respond with feedback. Encourage the student to continue practicing until he or she is confident enough to present the segment to the class.

Bridging: Prior to presenting the news report, allow each student time to practice with a small group. Have the student practice giving the full segment presentation to the group, and have the group respond to the presentation with feedback. Encourage the student to continue practicing until he or she is confident enough to present the segment to the class.

Part 3 Compelling Question ⏱ 10 minutes

After groups have finished presenting their news reports, encourage them to reflect on what they learned. As a class, discuss the compelling question for this Quest, "What forms the character of a region?"

Students have learned the specific things that form the character of a region, such as environmental factors, weather, industry, and tourism. They should use what they learned to answer the compelling question.

Part 4 Quest Reflection ⏱ 5 minutes

Materials: Student Activity Mat 4B Quest

After the completion of the Quest, have students complete the Student Activity Mat 4B Quest to reflect on the Quest activities. Call on volunteers to share their thoughts and reflections.

From the News Desk

The flu has struck the entire news crew of an Amarillo television news station. It's up to you to research and present the news to keep the regional viewers in the Southwest informed. Investigate to learn how the environment, weather, industries, and attractions contribute to the character of the region. Then use what you've learned to plan and present a newscast.

Your Mission:

The news never takes a sick day! Develop a newscast, complete with segments about the environment, weather, top industries, and local attractions for the viewers of the news station. Then fill in for the sick news crew and present your newscast to the viewers.

To prepare for your newscast:

Activity 1 **Our Environment Today and Tomorrow:** Research the importance of water conservation and include ten tips for the environmental news segment.

Activity 2 **Weather Report:** Determine typical climate and weather patterns for four Southwest cities to use in the weather segment.

Activity 3 **The Southwest Works:** Investigate one of the Southwest's top industries for a remote interview segment.

Activity 4 **Commercial Break:** Identify a local tourist attraction and create a 60-second commercial for your news program.

Complete Your Quest

Use your research and notes to develop and present the newscast with effective transitions between group members.

Activity 2

Name _____ Date _____

Weather Report

Use the map to record the average temperatures of four cities in the Southwest region. Record the typical weather patterns on the map for the four cities you chose.

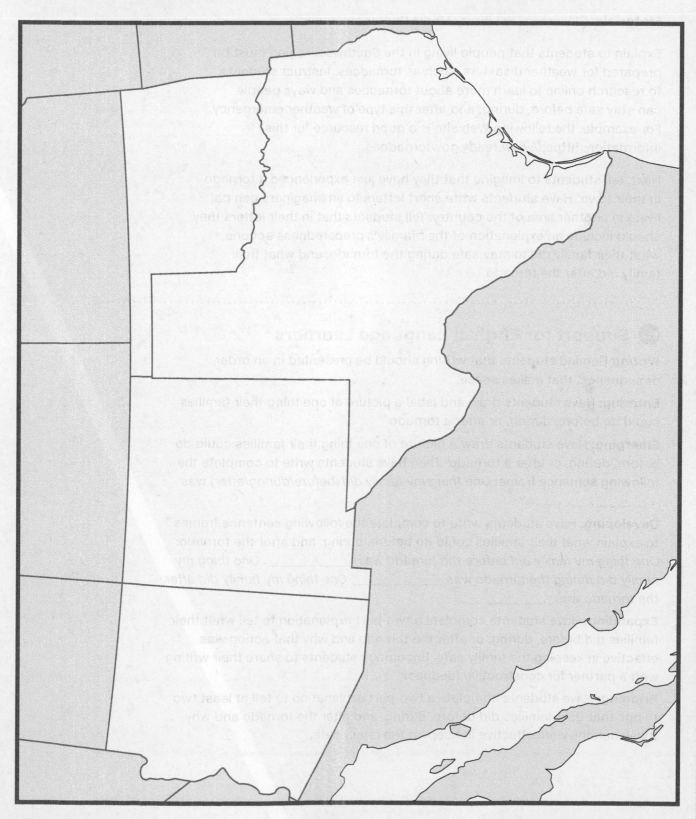

We Were Ready!

Individuals (20) **minutes**

Materials: Classroom or Library Media Center resources

Explain to students that people living in the Southwest region must be prepared for weather disasters, such as tornadoes. Instruct students to research online to learn more about tornadoes and ways people can stay safe before, during, and after this type of weather emergency. For example, the following Web site is a good resource for this information: https://www.ready.gov/tornadoes.

Next, tell students to imagine that they have just experienced a tornado in their town. Have students write short letters to an imaginary pen pal living in another area of the country. Tell students that in their letters they should include an explanation of their family's preparedness actions, what their family did to stay safe during the tornado, and what their family did after the tornado.

··

ELL Support for English Language Learners

Writing Remind students that writing should be presented in an order, or sequence, that makes sense.

Entering: Have students draw and label a picture of one thing their families could do before, during, or after a tornado.

Emerging: Have students draw a picture of one thing their families could do before, during, or after a tornado. Then have students write to complete the following sentence frame: *One thing my family did (before/during/after) was*

_____.

Developing: Have students write to complete the following sentence frames to explain what their families could do before, during, and after the tornado: *One thing my family did before the tornado was _____. One thing my family did during the tornado was _____. One thing my family did aft the tornado was _____.*

Expanding: Have students complete a two-part explanation to tell what *i* families did before, during, or after the tornado and why that action wa effective in keeping the family safe. Encourage students to share thei riting with a partner for constructive feedback.

Bridging: Have students complete a two-part explanation to tell at st two things that their families did before, during, and after the tornado d why these actions were effective in keeping the family safe.

Hopi Farming

Materials: Blackline Master: Hopi Farming

Explain to students that the Hopi are one of the oldest American Indian nations in the United States. Their farming techniques have been traditionally used throughout the centuries.

Distribute the blackline master **Hopi Farming,** which includes photos that show the farming techniques used by the Hopi. Instruct students to study each photo as you explain the technique.

- **Photo 1:** Flood plain farming—The Hopi planted crops in the flood plains of small streams. Seasonal flooding provided these crops with the additional water necessary to grow. They also planted crops at the mouths of small streams. At these mouths, wet soil was available.

- **Photo 2:** Sand dune farming—The Hopi used the desert sand to their advantage in sand dune farming. They created mounds of sand that directed water to the hard rock below. The water could not escape and was able to be used by the plant's roots.

Have students discuss these farming methods with a partner. Then have students respond to the questions on the blackline master.

Primary Source: The Grand Canyon

Individuals (20) minutes

Materials: Primary Source: The Grand Canyon, highlighters, Student Activity Mat 3B Time and Place

Explain to students that the Grand Canyon, one of the Seven Natural Wonders of the World, is located in Arizona. It is 277 miles long, up to a mile deep, and up to eighteen miles wide. Explain that the Grand Canyon was formed by the strong current of the Colorado River.

Distribute copies of **Primary Source: The Grand Canyon,** which includes an account from John Wesley Powell's journal describing the Grand Canyon from his expedition in 1869. Explain that Powell was the first known non–American Indian to ever lead an expedition through the Grand Canyon, and his words were chosen carefully to help his readers "see" this magnificent sight through his words. If necessary or desired, show students additional printed or online photos of the Grand Canyon in order to build background knowledge.

Have students read the primary source once before distributing highlighters to the students. Then have students read the primary source again, this time highlighting the descriptive words Powell used in order to give his readers a concept of the enormity of the Grand Canyon. Finally, have students use what they've learned to write their own descriptions of the Grand Canyon.

Encourage students to use Student Activity Mat 3B Time and Place to identify the location of the Grand Canyon and the year Powell lead his expedition. If time allows, encourage students to add two more points to their timeline and map outline based on prior knowledge and information.

Flags and Mottos

Materials: Blackline Master: Flags and Mottos, scissors, glue

Explain to students that states choose state flags and state mottos that they feel best represent their regions and the people who live there.

Distribute the blackline master **Flags and Mottos,** which include the mottos and state flags for states in the Southwest: Texas, Arizona, New Mexico, and Oklahoma.

Tell groups to look at the state flags and read the state mottos on the first page of the blackline master. Tell students to cut the flags and mottos and match them on the second page of the blackline master; however, instruct students not to glue them. As student groups work to determine their matches, tell them to study the flags closely and look for concepts or ideas that seem to match with a state's motto. Allow time for students to discuss and analyze their choices. Finally, review the matches with students and have them glue the correct matches on the second page of the blackline master.

Hopi Farming

Study the photos as your teacher discusses Hopi farming methods. Then, discuss the methods with a partner and work together to answer the questions.

1. Why did the Hopi develop these methods of farming?

_____

_____

2. How do these methods improve farming in a dry region?

_____

_____

Primary Source

Name _____   Date _____

The Grand Canyon

Read the primary source journal entry. Then, highlight the words and phrases with vivid descriptions.

> The walls now are more than a mile in height—
> a vertical distance difficult to appreciate . . .
> A thousand feet of this is up through granite
> crags; then steep slopes and perpendicular
> cliffs rise one above another to the summit . . .
> The gorge is black and narrow below, red and
> gray and flaring above, with crags and angular
> projections on the walls, which, cut in many
> places by side canyons, seem to be a vast
> wilderness of rocks.
>
> —John Wesley Powell, excerpt from *First Through
> the Grand Canyon*, 1869

Based on the primary source, write your own description of the Grand Canyon.

_____

_____

_____

_____

_____

_____

_____

_____

Flags and Mottos

Cut out the state flags and mottos. Discuss your ideas about matches
with your group.

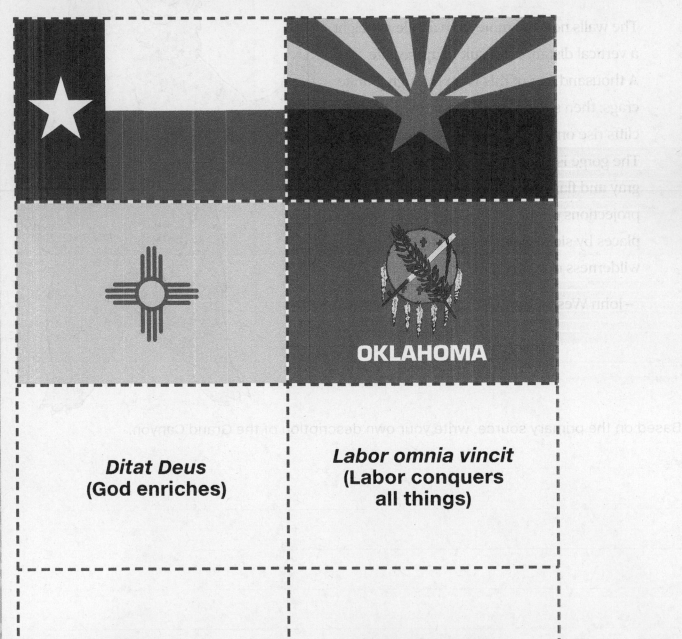

Ditat Deus
(God enriches)

Labor omnia vincit
**(Labor conquers
all things)**

Friendship

Crescit eundo
(It grows as it goes)

Place your matches on the spaces below. Do not glue in place until after you have discussed the matches with your teacher.

State	Flag	Motto
Texas:		
Arizona:		
New Mexico:		
Oklahoma:		

The Battle of the Alamo was an important battle in the Texas Revolution. As the army stationed at the Alamo watched the advance of the opposing Mexican army, their confidence in maintaining control of the site diminished. They battled day after day, each day hoping their reinforcements would arrive. As the days came and went with no help arriving, the soldiers grew more and more frustrated. They began to wonder if help was coming at all.

The Parts

3 players:

- **Davy Crockett,** famous frontiersman
- **William Travis,** lieutenant colonel
- **James Bowie,** colonel

Director's Notes:

Davy Crockett stands center stage as curtain opens. Other players appear on stage as directed.

Davy Crockett:
pacing back and forth, exasperated

I've been walking the hills and valleys of this frontier for years, and I don't ever remember it taking this long to get anywhere!

William Travis and James Bowie walk onstage to meet Davy Crockett.

Davy Crockett:

Well it's about time! I thought I'd never see our reinforcements get here.

William Travis:

Crockett, I presume?

Davy Crockett:

That's me.

James Bowie:

Commander Bowie, here. And this is Commander Travis.

Both men pause to shake hands with Davy Crockett.

Regions: The Southwest
Readers Theater

Davy Crockett: Well forgive my social disgraces, but right now I don't care who you are. I'm just glad to see somebody here!

William Travis: We received word of your need for reinforcements. We brought men with us to aid in securing the Alamo.

Davy Crockett stands on tiptoes, and places a hand over his eyes, as though peering into the distance over the shoulders of Travis and Bowie.

Davy Crockett: Great, but where are they?

James Bowie: Well, right there, of course.
turning around, pointing behind himself

Davy Crockett: Right there? Right there, he says. Right there.
shaking head in disbelief

William Travis: Mr. Crockett, is there a problem?

Davy Crockett: A problem? A problem! We're being attacked by thousands of
shouting, pacing back   Mexican soldiers and you two show up here with fewer than a
and forth   hundred men and want to know if there's a problem?

James Bowie: Mr. Crockett, our reinforcements are highly trained and ready
raising his eyebrows   to fight in the war for independence for Texas.

Davy Crockett takes a deep breath and lets it out slowly.

Davy Crockett: I know they are. I just thought, when they said they'd
calmer, head lowered   send reinforcements that they'd send, you know, major reinforcements.

From offstage, a loud cannon booms. Shouting can be heard in the distance. All three players drop to their knees and cover their heads.

Davy Crockett: It's another attack! Take cover!

The three players crawl offstage as booming cannons and shouting echo from offstage.

After a few moments, the three men stagger back onstage.

James Bowie:
Mr. Crockett, I can now understand your reaction at our arrival. We are not prepared to defeat a Mexican army of this size. We must have more help.

Davy Crockett:
If we don't . . . I don't know how we'll succeed.

William Travis:
I'll write a letter at once. We must have more reinforcements.

William Travis walks offstage and returns with a pen and paper. He mimics writing as he reads his lines.

William Travis:
To the people of Texas and all Americans in the world. We are under attack by at least a thousand men, if not more. The Mexican army has demanded our surrender. We have refused and our flag still waves proudly. I will never surrender. I call on all of you who hold to the truths of liberty and patriotism to aid us. The Mexican army receives new soldiers daily, and they will soon grow large enough to overtake us easily. If this letter is ignored, I pledge to fight as long as I can and to die with the honor of serving my country. In victory or in death, William Travis.

James Bowie:
nods with respect
That letter will certainly spur others to join us in our fight.

Davy Crockett:
I sure hope so.

William Travis:
I'll have my most trusted ranger, Captain Albert Martin, make sure this letter reaches its destination. The people must respond. They must.

Davy Crockett:
Until they do, it's up to us.

The three men turn and walk offstage. End scene.

Objectives

- Identify landforms that can be seen in Yellowstone National Park.
- Analyze primary sources related to the California gold rush and the Klondike gold rush.
- Write an "I Was There" first-person narrative about a visit to Hawaii.
- Identify the locations of four iconic places in Los Angeles.

Quest Project-Based Learning: Go West!

	Description	Duration	Materials	Participants
STEP 1 Set the Stage	Read a blackline master as an introduction to the project.	15 minutes	**Blackline Master:** Quest Kick Off	Whole Class
STEP 2 Launch the Activities	Make relevant connections and build content background for the Quest.	5 minutes	**Leveled Readers:** *What's It Like in the West?; Life in the West; Exploring the West*	Whole Class
Activity 1 Yellowstone National Park	Analyze a map and identify landforms in Yellowstone National Park.	20 minutes	**Blackline Master:** Yellowstone National Park	Individual
Activity 2 **Primary Source:** Gold Rush	Evaluate advertisements for the California gold rush and the Klondike gold rush.	40 minutes	**Primary Source:** Gold Rush, Venn Diagram graphic organizer, classroom or Library Media Center resources	Individual
Activity 3 ELL Hawaiian Plants and Wildlife	Take an online tour of Hawaii and write a first-person narrative about your visit.	25 minutes	Classroom or Library Media Center resources	Individual
Activity 4 Los Angeles	Research four cultural attractions in Los Angeles.	15 minutes	**Blackline Master:** Los Angeles, classroom or Library Media Center resources	Individual
STEP 3 Complete the Quest Assemble Your Tourism Booklet	Create a colorful cover and compile completed Quest materials into a tourism booklet.	40 minutes	Completed Quest materials, Student Activity Mat 1B United States Outline, art supplies	Individual
Answer the **Compelling Question**	Discuss the compelling question.	15 minutes		Whole Class
Quest Reflection	Summarize the Quest activities and findings.	5 minutes	Student Activity Mat 4B Quest	Individual, Whole Class

Quick Activities

	Description	Duration	Materials	Participants
Western State Rap	Compose a rap about the landforms and climate of a state in the West.	20 minutes	Classroom or Library Media Center resources	Individual
Alaska's Industries	Analyze a circle graph about Alaska's industries.	30 minutes	**Blackline Master:** Alaska's Industries	Individual
Crossword Puzzle ELL	Create a crossword puzzle using the names of some American Indian groups as well as some historically significant individuals from the history of the West.	15 minutes	Classroom or Library Media Center resources, graph paper	Small Groups
Pacific Rim Trade	Research a product that is made in the western United States and exported to a country in the Pacific Rim.	20 minutes	**Blackline Master:** Pacific Rim Trade, classroom or Library Media Center resources, Student Activity Mat 3A Graphic Organizer	Partners
Read Aloud: European Explorers of the West	Read about Juan Rodriguez Cabrillo and Captain James Cook.	30 minutes	**Read Aloud:** European Explorers of the West	Small Groups

Project-Based Learning: Go West!

QCompelling**uestion** ## How can you convince visitors to listen to the old saying, "Go West!"?

Welcome to Quest 9, Go West! In this Quest, your students will study all aspects of the West region and then use what they learn to create an illustrated tourism booklet that encourages tourists to visit the West. Their booklets will explore the region's landforms, history, wildlife, and cities. After participating in the Quest activities, students will be prepared to discuss the compelling question at the end of this inquiry.

Objectives

- Identify landforms that can be seen in Yellowstone National Park.
- Analyze primary sources related to the California gold rush and the Klondike gold rush.
- Write an "I Was There" first-person narrative about a visit to Hawaii.
- Identify the locations of four iconic places in Los Angeles.

STEP 1 Set the Stage ⏱15 minutes

Begin the Quest by distributing the blackline master **Quest Kick Off.** It will bring the world of the Quest to life, introducing a story to interest students and a mission to motivate them.

Story

A well-known tourism company is struggling to get people to visit the states in western United States. The company's board of directors has asked students to create a tourism booklet that focuses on the West and all its fantastic features. The company will use the booklets to encourage people to "Go West!"

Mission

Students will create a colorful illustrated booklet called "Go West!" In it, they will show interesting places that make the West worth visiting.

STEP 2 Launch the Activities

The following four activities will help students prepare to create their tourism booklets by guiding them through four aspects of the West: its landforms, its history, its wildlife, and its cities.

Note that all four activities can be done independently of the larger Quest. As you begin, give students an opportunity to build content background as a launch into the following activities. Ask students what they know about the West and how it relates to the tourism industry.

Assign the appropriate Leveled Reader for this chapter.

Activity 1 Yellowstone National Park (20) **minutes**

Materials: Blackline Master: Yellowstone National Park

Copy and distribute the blackline master **Yellowstone National Park.** Explain that Yellowstone National Park is one of the most beautiful and extraordinary national parks in the United States. Tell students that it lies in three western states: Wyoming, Montana, and Idaho.

Ask students to study the map. Have them look for examples of the following landforms: rivers, lakes, geysers, hot springs, falls, and mountain peaks. Use the following definitions if students are unfamiliar with these terms:

- hot spring: a place where hot, natural water comes from the ground; the water is usually warmer than 98°F and is heated by hot or molten rock

- geyser: a hot, underground spring that shoots steam and boiling water high into the air

Support them as they write examples of each landform that they find on the map. As they do this, students are likely to find examples of landforms that may not use the name of the landform; for example, Old Faithful is a geyser, and the Kepler Cascades are falls. Encourage them to ask questions about these kinds of names as they encounter them.

Materials: Primary Source: Gold Rush, Venn Diagram graphic
organizer, classroom or Library Media Center resources

Copy and distribute the two-page blackline master **Primary Source: Gold Rush.**
Explain to students that a gold rush is when many people quickly move to an area
where gold has been discovered.

The most well-known gold rush took place in California in 1849, near present-day
Sacramento and San Francisco. Gold was discovered the previous year by James
Marshall at Sutter's Mill. Another famous gold rush in the West region took place
in the late 1890s, when gold was discovered in the Yukon region of Alaska. That
gold rush is known as the Klondike gold rush. Both events (and the California
gold rush in particular) are very significant in the history of the West because they
resulted in the population of the region increasing rapidly.

Have students analyze the two primary sources. The first is an advertisement for
people in the eastern United States to travel to San Francisco to participate in the
California gold rush. The second shows an ad for people who wanted to go to
Alaska during the Klondike gold rush.

Ask students to use classroom or Library Media Center resources to visit the official
Web sites of the Klondike gold rush National Historical Park (go to www.nps.gov and
search under "Alaska" for "Klondike Gold Rush") and the Marshall Gold Discovery
State Historic Park (go to www.parks.ca.gov and click "Visit a Park," then "Find a
Park," and look under the letter M). As they read about the history of the two gold rush
events, have them write their answers to these two questions on the blackline master:

- In what way (or ways) is this historic park interesting?

- Why should people visit this historic park?

Then copy and distribute the Venn Diagram graphic organizer from the back of the
workbook. Have students complete the Venn diagram with ways that the California
and Klondike gold rushes are similar and different, based on the text and the
primary source advertisements.

Provide students with support as they analyze the primary sources. For the
California advertisement, explain that Pier 13 East River and the Tontine Building
were locations in New York City. For the Klondike advertisement, explain that Pier
26 North River was a location in New York, and St. Michael and Dawson City were
locations in Alaska.

Activity 3 | Hawaiian Plants and Wildlife (25) minutes

Materials: Classroom or Library Media Center resources

Explain that the state of Hawaii is part of the West region. Hawaii has some of the most interesting and beautiful plants and wildlife of any state. Tell them that there are special places called refuges where people can see wildlife. At a botanical garden, people can see plants and flowers.

Ask students to use classroom or Library Media Center resources to visit two Web sites: the Hawaiian Islands National Wildlife Refuge (https://www.fws.gov/refuge/Hawaiian_Islands and click on "Wildlife & Habitat") and the Hawaii Tropical Botanical Garden (http://hawaiigarden.com and click on "The Garden Trails" to go on a virtual tour). Students will learn more about Hawaii's unique wildlife and plant life.

Ask students to write a two-paragraph first-person narrative about one of the two places. It should be an "I Was There" story, as if each student actually visited the place. Have students describe what they saw, felt, and experienced. Also, they should give reasons why tourists should visit there.

ELL Support for English Language Learners

Writing Support students as they write a first-person narrative about one of the places in Hawaii they "visited" online.

Entering: Explain to students that in their narratives, they should start many sentences with the pronoun *I*. Write the following sentence frame on the board: _____ *saw the Nihoa finch at the Hawaiian Islands National Wildlife Refuge.* Ask for volunteers to come up to the board and fill in the blank with the pronoun *I*.

Emerging: Write the following sentence frame on the board: *I saw _____ at the Hawaiian Islands National Wildlife Refuge/Hawaii Tropical Botanical Garden.* Ask for volunteers to fill in the blank with something they "saw" there.

Developing: Draw a three-column graphic organizer on the board with the heads "Saw," "Felt," and "Experienced." Ask students to write one thing in one of the columns based on the Web site they browsed. Explain how they can use the graphic organizer to support the writing of an *I* statement in their narrative.

Expanding: Draw a three-column graphic organizer on the board with the heads "Saw," "Felt," and "Experienced." Ask students to fill in two columns based on the Web site they browsed. Then ask them to write an *I* statement for each thing they wrote in the graphic organizer.

Bridging: Draw a three-column graphic organizer on the board with the heads "Saw," "Felt," and "Experienced." Ask students to fill in all three columns based on the Web site they browsed. Then have students practice writing *I* statements for each of the three things they wrote in the graphic organizer.

Materials: Blackline Master: Los Angeles, classroom or Library
Media Center resources

Explain to students that the West is home to some of the most interesting cities
in the United States. One such city is Los Angeles, California. Los Angeles is the
second-largest city in the United States in terms of population. It is culturally very
diverse and is home to sunny beaches, outstanding museums and concert halls,
and, of course, Hollywood. Explain to students that Hollywood is an area of Los
Angeles, and it is the center of filmmaking for the entire world.

Distribute copies of blackline master **Los Angeles** to students. Explain that they
will be researching the location of four cultural attractions of the city: Santa Monica
State Beach, the Chinese Theater, the Walt Disney Concert Hall, and the J. Paul
Getty Museum. Have students use classroom or Library Media Center resources to
research and identify where each iconic place is located on the illustrated map.

STEP 3 Complete the *Quest*

Part 1 Assemble Your Tourism Booklet ⟨40⟩ minutes

Materials: Completed Quest materials, Student Activity Mat 1B United States Outline, art supplies

As a first step in their assembly of their tourism booklet, distribute Student Activity Mat 1B United States Outline to students, which will serve as the first page of their completed booklet. Have students color in the states that are part of the West region. Then have them label the following places they learned about:

- Yellowstone National Park

- Marshall Gold Discovery State Historic Park

- Klondike Gold Rush National Historical Park

- Hawaiian Islands National Wildlife Refuge

- Hawaii Tropical Botanical Garden

- Los Angeles, California

Next, distribute art supplies and have students design a colorful front cover. Then have them put their pages in order, beginning with their completed Student Activity Mat 1B United States Outline, then the blackline master for Activity 1, two blackline masters and a Venn diagram for Activity 2, their first-person narrative for Activity 3, and the blackline master for Activity 4. Provide students with a sturdy back cover. Finally, students should assemble their booklets using a three-hole punch and brass fasteners.

Part 2 Compelling Question ⟨15⟩ minutes

After students complete their tourism booklets, encourage them to reflect on what they learned. As a class, discuss the compelling question for this Quest, "How can you convince visitors to listen to the old saying, 'Go West!'?"

Students have learned about the region's landforms, history, wildlife, and cities. They should use what they learned to answer the compelling question.

Part 3 Quest Reflection ⟨5⟩ minutes

Materials: Student Activity Mat 4B Quest

To provide closure, have students complete the boxes on the Student Activity Mat 4B Quest. Ask volunteers to share a few of their responses aloud.

Go West!

A tourism company is trying to get people to visit every region of the United States, but no one seems interested in traveling to the West. The company is asking you to create an illustrated tourism booklet about this beautiful region. The company will use your booklet to encourage tourists to "Go West!"

Your Mission

Create your own illustrated tourism booklet about the West. Your booklet will highlight the region's landforms, history, wildlife, and cities.

To gather information for your booklet:

Activity 1 **Yellowstone National Park:** Identify landforms inside Yellowstone National Park.

Activity 2 **Gold Rush:** Study advertisements for the California gold rush and the Klondike gold rush.

Activity 3 **Hawaiian Plants and Wildlife:** Research Hawaiian plants and wildlife in order to write about an imaginary visit to Hawaii.

Activity 4 **Los Angeles:** Research and find the locations of four iconic places in Los Angeles.

Complete Your Quest

Create an illustrated tourism booklet about the West region.

Yellowstone National Park

Yellowstone National Park is one of the West's most beautiful places to visit. Study the map and the map legend. Identify some of the landforms that can be found in the park. Then, write down a specific example of each landform.

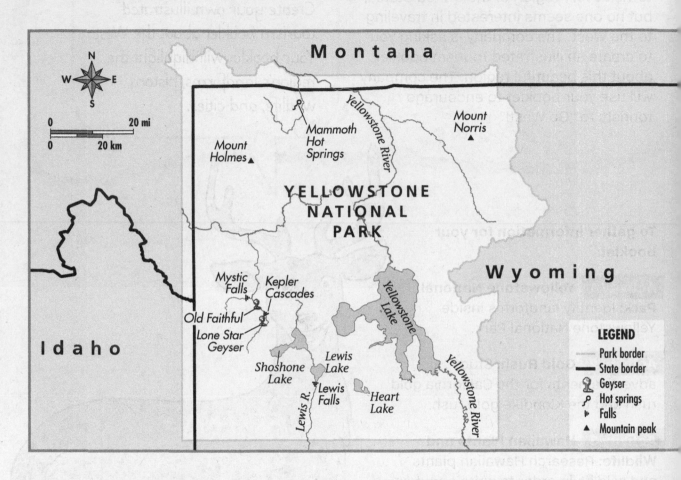

rivers _____

hot springs _____

lakes _____

falls _____

geysers _____

mountain peaks _____

Gold Rush

In 1848, gold was discovered in California at Sutter's Mill near the present-day city of Sacramento. The news spread quickly, and thousands of people came to California in hopes of finding gold and becoming rich. People living in the eastern part of the United States needed a way to get to California, and soon companies were advertising trips aboard fast ships called clippers. Clipper ships took people from eastern cities like New York to San Francisco, which was the closest port to the gold rush.

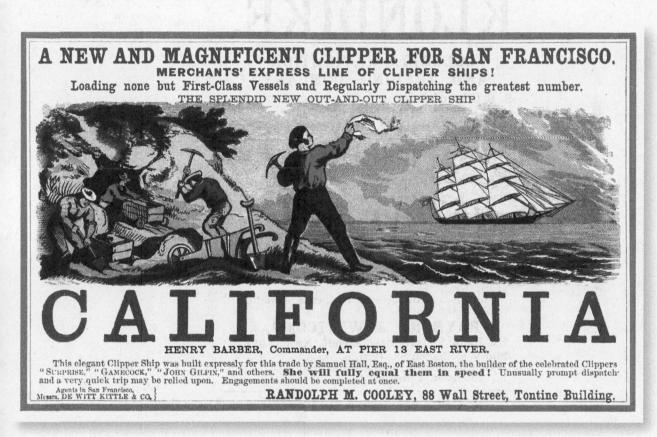

Follow your teacher's instructions and visit the Marshall Gold Discovery State Historic Park Web site. In what way (or ways) is this historic park interesting? Why should people visit this historic park? Write down your answers.

_____

_____

_____

_____

Another gold rush took place in the 1890s in Alaska. Gold was discovered in the area where the Klondike and Yukon Rivers meet. Thousands of people rushed there in hopes of finding riches. Companies sold trips on sailing ships (known as barks) from San Francisco, California, to Alaska.

How to reach the
KLONDIKE.

COLUMBIA NAVIGATION
AND TRADING COMPANY.

S. S. City of Columbia (1900 tons) will depart from the Old Dominion Line Pier 26, North River,

Wednesday, Dec. 1st, for

ST. MICHAEL,

connecting with Company's river steamers for

DAWSON CITY.

Fare to Dawson City, including 1000 pounds of baggage, $680.00 up, according to accommodation. Passengers desiring to meet the ship at San Francisco or Seattle will be provided with transportation by rail to either point at same rate.

For passage tickets and further information apply to the agents,

RAYMOND & WHITCOMB,
31 East Fourteenth Street, New York.

296 Washington St., Boston, Mass.
1005 Chestnut St., Philadelphia, Pa.
95 Adams St., Chicago, Ill.

Now visit the Web site of the Klondike Gold Rush National Historic Park. In what way (or ways) is the historic park interesting? Why should people visit this historic park? Write down your answers.

_____

_____

_____

_____

Los Angeles

Name _____ Date _____

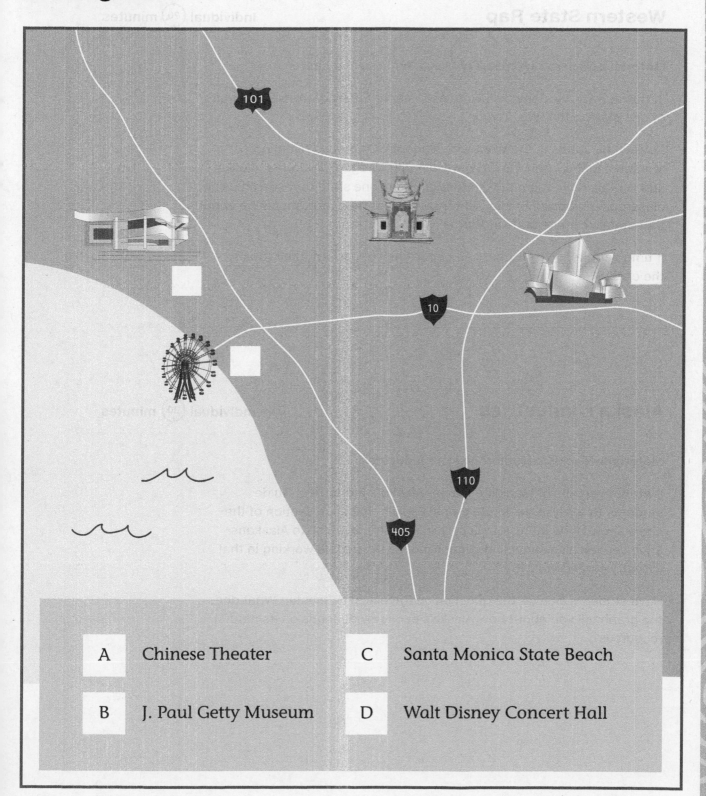

A	Chinese Theater	C	Santa Monica State Beach
B	J. Paul Getty Museum	D	Walt Disney Concert Hall

Quick Activities

Western State Rap

Materials: Classroom or Library Media Center resources

In this activity, students will write a rap about the landforms and climate of one state in the West region.

Review the states in the West with students: Colorado, Wyoming, Montana, Idaho, Utah, Nevada, Washington, Oregon, California, Alaska, and Hawaii. Have them pick (or assign them) one state to research using classroom or Library Media Center resources. Their raps should be about that state's climate and landforms.

If time permits, give students an opportunity to perform their raps for the class.

Alaska's Industries

Individual (30) minutes

Materials: Blackline Master: Alaska's Industries

Distribute copies of blackline master **Alaska's Industries.** Guide students to analyze the circle graph. Explain that each section of the circle shows how many jobs a certain industry provides to Alaskans. Each section also shows how much money the people working in that industry earned in 2015.

Have students answer the question on the blackline master: What does the graph tell you about how Alaska's economy depends on its natural resources?

Crossword Puzzle

Materials: Classroom or Library Media Center resources, graph paper

Explain to students that they will be making a crossword puzzle using the names of some American Indian groups as well as some historically significant individuals from the history of the West. Divide the students into small groups. Distribute graph paper.

Write the following terms on the board: Tlingit, Inuit, Blackfeet, Chumash, Polynesians, Cabrillo, Serra, Smith, Marshall, Sutter, Hirono.

Have each group choose four of these terms to include in their crossword puzzle. Show students a sample crossword puzzle from the newspaper or the Internet and demonstrate how it is solved. Have students use it as a model for making their own puzzle. Have students research the terms in order to write clues for their crossword. Have groups trade puzzles with each other and try to solve them.

• •

(ELL) Support for English Language Learners

Writing Support students as they write clues for their crossword puzzles.

Entering: Explain to students that crossword clues should be as short and succinct as possible, but still provide enough information. Write the following crossword clues on the board, supposing your last name was the correct answer: teacher; your teacher; last name of your fourth-grade teacher. Ask a volunteer to circle the clue that is the shortest but gives enough information. (your teacher)

Emerging: Explain to students that crossword clues should be as short and succinct as possible, but still provide enough information. Ask students to work in pairs to come up with a crossword clue that would result in your last name as the correct answer.

Developing: Explain to students that crossword clues can be humorous and have words that sound the same. Write the following crossword clue on the board: also a girl's name. Ask a volunteer to underline the term that sounds the same as the name *Sarah*. (Serra)

Expanding: Explain to students that crossword clues can be humorous and often contain wordplay. Write the following crossword clue on the board: a similar term for bog + when you count everything. Then point to the term *Marshall* on the board. Ask a volunteer to circle the clue words that help to identify the term.

Bridging: Explain to students that crossword clues can use multiple meanings of words. Write the following crossword clue on the board: works with metal. Ask a volunteer to underline the term that means the same thing as the word *blacksmith*. (Smith)

Pacific Rim Trade

Partners (20) minutes

Materials: Blackline Master: Pacific Rim Trade, classroom or Library Media Center resources, Student Activity Mat 3A Graphic Organizer

Distribute copies of blackline master **Pacific Rim Trade.** Explain to students that the map shows goods that are exported from countries that border the Pacific Ocean. Define *export* for students as "something that is sold or traded to another country." For example, according to the map and the map legend, the United States exports automobiles and aircraft. All the nations that face the Pacific Ocean trade with each other.

Ask student pairs to pick one product that the United States exports (according to the map) and use classroom or Library Media Center resources to research the following:

- which state in the West it is manufactured in

- one country that the product is exported to

Distribute Student Activity Mat 3A Graphic Organizer. Encourage students to use the graphic organizer as an outline for their notes. Tell students to write the name of the product in the first box. In the second box, have students write the state the product is manufactured in, and for the third box, have students write the country the product is exported to. Have students add supporting details inside each box.

When all students have finished, lead a class discussion about what they learned.

Alaska's Industries

Analyze the circle graph. Then answer the question.

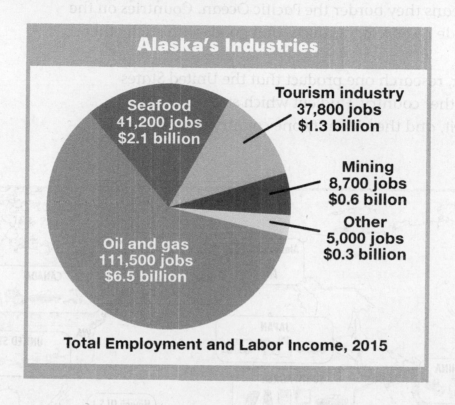

Alaska's Industries

Seafood
41,200 jobs
$2.1 billion

Tourism industry
37,800 jobs
$1.3 billion

Mining
8,700 jobs
$0.6 billon

Other
5,000 jobs
$0.3 billion

Oil and gas
111,500 jobs
$6.5 billion

Total Employment and Labor Income, 2015

What does the graph tell you about how Alaska's economy depends on its natural resources?
Explain your answer.

_____

_____

_____

_____

_____

_____

_____

Pacific Rim Trade

Analyze the map. You will notice it shows countries on the Pacific Rim, which means they border the Pacific Ocean. Countries on the Pacific Rim trade resources, products, and goods with each other.

With a partner, research one product that the United States exports to another country. Find out which state in the West manufactures it, and then identify one country that the product is exported to.

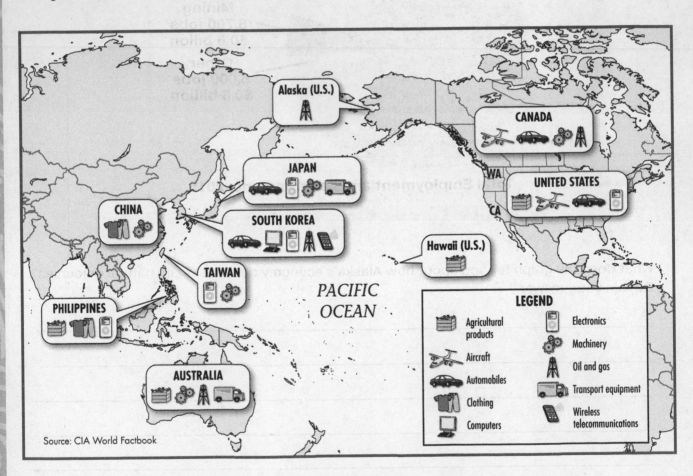

Source: CIA World Factbook

The voyages of Christopher Columbus that began in 1492 set off a long period of European exploration in the Americas. Columbus was sailing on behalf of the king and queen of Spain. Spain was looking for a new route from Europe to Asia that would make trade easier.

In 1535, Spain established a colony in the Americas that they named New Spain. New Spain included present-day Mexico and Central America. The colony was run by Spanish officials and soldiers, and people from Spain went there to settle the land.

In 1542, the official in charge of New Spain asked an explorer named Juan Rodriguez Cabrillo to sail north along the coast of the Pacific Ocean from present-day Mexico toward what would someday become California. Cabrillo set out with three ships and a diverse crew of about 200 soldiers and sailors, some of whom were American Indians from Mexico. Cabrillo's crew probably included some enslaved Africans as well.

About 100 days after they began their journey, Cabrillo and his crew reached what is now San Diego Bay, in southern California. Cabrillo claimed the land for Spain. Then he and his crew continued north, up the coast, battling strong winds and ocean currents. They stopped at islands along the way and met the Chumash, an American Indian group. A member of Cabrillo's crew recorded his thoughts about the Chumash:

The Indians brought . . . many sardines [fish], fresh and very good. They say that in the interior there are many pueblos [villages] and abundant [much] food. They ate no maize [corn]. They were dressed in skins, and wore their hair very long and tied up with long strings . . .

By the time the Cabrillo expedition was complete, Cabrillo himself had died. However, Juan Rodriguez Cabrillo is remembered as the first European to explore the coast of California. He was also the first European to visit California from the sea, rather than over land. Cabrillo also made the first reports of American Indians living in California.

Spain continued to send explorers along the Pacific coast for a number of years, but they showed little interest in settling California. What little they had seen of the land did not impress them. Also, traveling by land over deserts and mountains was difficult. Harsh winds and ocean currents made sea travel difficult, too, as Juan Rodriguez Cabrillo had learned. Settling California was simply not a priority for Spain.

However, by the mid-1700s, other European countries began to show interest in California, which got Spain's attention.

A British explorer named Captain James Cook had long been a successful explorer for Britain. He had traveled the areas around present-day New Zealand and Australia, as well as the frozen continent of Antarctica.

In the winter of 1778, Cook was exploring the northern parts of the Pacific Ocean when he landed on the Hawaiian Islands. He was the first European to make contact with Hawaii. He continued his voyage to the east, eventually exploring the coast of California, but north of where Spain had its settlements. He eventually landed in present-day Oregon and continued up along the coast of Canada and Alaska.

Like Juan Rodriguez Cabrillo, Captain James Cook is remembered as an important European explorer. He was the first European to land in both Oregon and Hawaii, among other accomplishments.

K-W-L Chart

What We **K**now	What We **W**ant to Know	What We **L**earned

Web

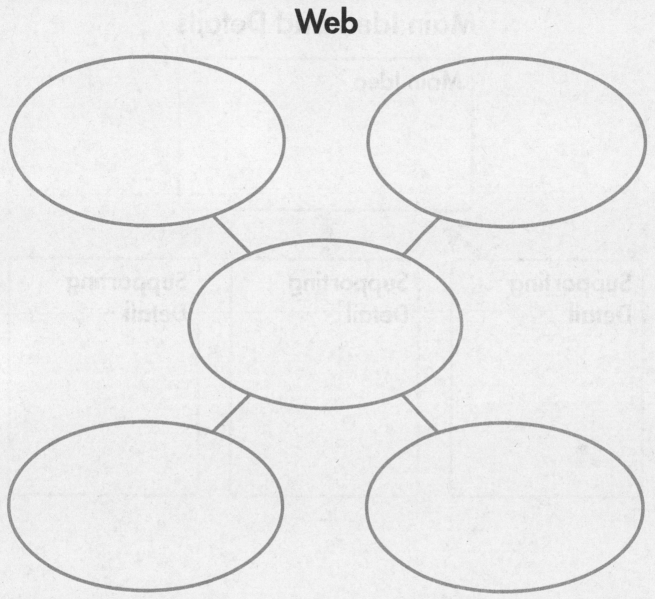

Main Idea and Details

Main Idea

Supporting Detail

Supporting Detail

Supporting Detail

Venn Diagram

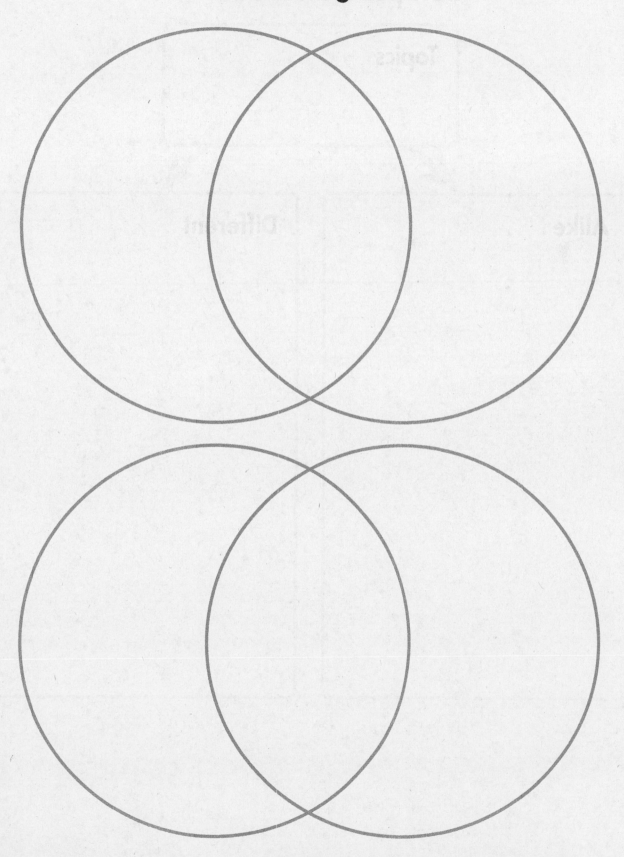

Compare and Contrast

Topics

Alike	Different

Cause and Effect

Causes	Effects

Why did it happen?

What happened?

Why did it happen?

What happened?

Why did it happen?

What happened?

Problem and Solution A

Problem

Solution

Problem and Solution B

Problem

⬇

How I Tried to Solve the Problem

⬇

Solution

Steps in a Process A

Process

....

....

```
┌─────────────────────────────────────┐
│                                       │
│  Step 1                               │
│                                       │
│                                       │
└─────────────────────────────────────┘
                  ↓
┌─────────────────────────────────────┐
│                                       │
│  Step 2                               │
│                                       │
│                                       │
└─────────────────────────────────────┘
                  ↓
┌─────────────────────────────────────┐
│                                       │
│  Step 3                               │
│                                       │
│                                       │
└─────────────────────────────────────┘
```

Steps in a Process B

Process

....

....

```
┌──────────────────────────────────────────────┐
│                                                │
│  Step 1                                         │
│                                                │
│                                                │
└──────────────────────────────────────────────┘
                        ↓
┌──────────────────────────────────────────────┐
│                                                │
│  Step 2                                         │
│                                                │
│                                                │
└──────────────────────────────────────────────┘
                        ↓
┌──────────────────────────────────────────────┐
│                                                │
│  Step 3                                         │
│                                                │
│                                                │
└──────────────────────────────────────────────┘
                        ↓
┌──────────────────────────────────────────────┐
│                                                │
│  Step 4                                         │
│                                                │
│                                                │
└──────────────────────────────────────────────┘
```

T-Chart

Three-Column Chart

Four-Column Chart

Outline Form

Title

....

....

A. ....

   1. ....

   2. ....

   3. ....

B. ....

   1. ....

   2. ....

   3. ....

C. ....

   1. ....

   2. ....

   3. ....

Answer Key

Chapter 1

Quick Activity: Water Cycle Collage, p. 18

Students should glue appropriate labels on the mountain stream, the clouds in the sky, and the lake. They should also affix the Precipitation label on or near the bottom right arrow. The arrow on the bottom left should be labeled Evaporation, and the arrow at the top should be labeled Condensation.

Quick Activity: Resources Word Search, p. 19

Key:

_____ = red

_____ = blue

.... = green

```
K K B Z K D F Q A J S S Z L Y
S M I E N L A X Y X W R U O O
R C D S R O R Z V Q G M I T J
R R M M X G M H G L B J O K Y
E N U A O P E A I E A N F B O
T J L G S A R O R N K I W X T
U D H O N Y S R S J T P B C P
P L O C Q F P D Q C A M E R A
M G A C L E V O H S T C X R I
O H K O T F V Q K R M Z E N A
C R W P C O S X K Q Y H N A P
V U M O F E R A D H C V U C V
G Q G J O Z Q Z M A C W Y C L
T T J M G T K P E M K N H J F
Y P Z Y J X Q T R E S Z R M B
```

Chapter 2

Quick Activity: Columbian Exchange Vote, p. 39

Corn (N. America), Apples (Europe), Wheat (Europe), Turkeys (N. America), Potatoes (N. America), Chocolate (N. America), Cows (Europe)

Quick Activity: Primary Source: Migrant Mother, p. 41

Possible answer: The mother in this picture looks sad and upset. She looks like she is very tired and wants something very badly.

Possible answer: The family's clothes are torn and ragged. It looks like their hair is messy and dirty. They look like they live in a tent.

Possible answer: I think Lange was trying to show that there are a lot of families like this family. The Great Depression and the dust storms during the 1930s affected a lot of people. Many people suffered during this time.

Chapter 3

Quick Activity: How a Bill Becomes a Law, p. 60

Both sides of the infographic, reading from the top down, should have the following labels: <u>bill</u>, [committee], <u>vote</u>. The box below "conference committee" should be labeled <u>vote</u>. At the bottom of the infographic, labels should read as follows, from left to right: <u>veto</u>, <u>president</u>, <u>law</u>.

Chapter 4

Quest Activity 4: Primary Source: Analyze an Advertisement, p. 75

(Possible answers:)

Blue underline: *Delicately Scented; White Rose; Soothing—Beneficial*

Yellow highlight: *Competition has not touched it; That Means Merit*

Sample Testimonial: *I use White Rose Glycerine Soap every day. My skin is so smooth. I love smelling like I've been walking in a rose garden.*

Quick Activity 3: Supply and Demand, p. 81

Possible answers:

1. The law of supply and demand says that there is a relationship between how much of a product is available (the supply) and how much of a product consumers want to buy (demand).
2. The price goes up.
3. The price goes down.

Quick Activity 4: Opportunity Cost, p. 82

Possible answers:

1. I would buy the stuffed animal.
2. I would like to buy the hardcover book.
3. The opportunity cost is the value of the item I want to buy. In this case, it would be $12.00.

Chapter 5

Quest Activity 1: Mapping Maples, p. 93

Students should color the states as indicated below:

State	Color
Connecticut	Red
Maine	Green
Massachusetts	Orange
New Hampshire	Yellow
New York	Blue
Pennsylvania	Yellow
Vermont	Purple

Quest Activity 2: Maple FAQ, p. 94

Possible answers:

1. Maple syrup is made from the sap of the sugar maple tree.
2. Sap is removed from trees by a process called tapping, where a cut or hole is made in the tree during late winter or early spring, when it is warm during the day and cold at night.

3. Tapping leaves a wound on the tree, but the tree can heal from it, so no harm is done.

4. Tapping must be done in late winter or early spring because a period of freezing followed by a period of thawing is required. Daytime temperatures must warm enough that the sap can flow freely.

5. There is no exact figure for how much maple syrup can be made from one tree, but one tree typically produces 10 to 20 gallons of sap, and it takes about 40 gallons of sap to produce one gallon of maple syrup. Therefore, a good estimate is ¼ to ½ gallon per tree.

6. No, pancake syrup is not the same as maple syrup. Pancake syrup is usually made from high fructose corn syrup, not the sap of maple trees.

Quick Activity 3: Famous Authors From the Northeast, p. 99

Writer	Location	Famous Works
Zora Neale Hurston	Notasulga, AL (birth); lived New York, NY & Westfield, NJ; Fort Pierce, FL (death)	*Their Eyes Were Watching God, Moses, Man of the Mountain*
Nathaniel Hawthorne	Salem, MA (birth); lived various places including MA & ME, Plymouth, NH (death)	*The House of the Seven Gables; The Scarlet Letter*
Ralph Waldo Emerson	Boston, MA (birth); Concord, MA (death)	"Nature"; "Self-Reliance"; *Essays: First Series*
Stephen King	Portland, ME (birth); lived Bangor, ME	*Carrie, The Shining, It, The Stand*
Emily Dickinson	Amherst, MA (birth & death)	"I'm Nobody! Who are you?"; "'Hope' is the thing with feathers"; "Because I could not stop for Death"; "A Bird, came down the Walk"
Julia Alvarez	Middlebury and Burlington, Vermont; Andover, Massachusetts; Wilmington, Delaware	*How Tía Lola Saved the Summer; Return to Sender*
Louisa May Alcott	Germantown, PA (birth); lived Boston, MA & Concord, MA; Boston, MA (death)	*Little Women; Little Men; Jo's Boys*

Chapter 6

Quest Activity 4: The Civil Rights Era, p. 116

Possible answer: John Lewis is asking for higher pay for African American workers, their right to protest peacefully, and their right to vote.

Quick Activity: World Heritage Sites, p. 121

Question 1: Answers will vary, but students should identify unique and significant details about the site they chose.

Question 2: Answers will vary, but students will likely reference the unique and significant details they identified.

Quick Activity: Primary Source: George Washington Carver, p. 122

Possible answer: Carver is old and wearing a lab coat; he is working by himself; he looks like he is concentrating very hard; he is surrounded by glass jars; it appears that his work is very technical.

Quick Activity: Land of the South, p. 123

Students should draw arrows in the first stanza connecting *land* with *hand*, *rise* with *skies*, *these* with *me*, and *roam* with *home*. In the second stanza, they should draw arrows connecting *wealth* with *health*, *sea* with *be*, *streams* with *thee*, and *dome* with *home*.

Students' discussions will vary, but they should be sure to mention the landforms and physical characteristics of the Southeast that the poem mentions, including its mountains, fields, rivers, hills, valleys, and so forth.

Chapter 7

Quick Activity: Inside a Tornado, p. 145

1. Students should circle "Sandy Latimer has always been unusually terrified of thunderstorms."

2. Students should underline any two sentences from the first paragraph.

3. Possible answer: A woman with a lifelong fear of storms found out just how terrifying they can be when she was caught in a tornado.

4. Possible answers: fear, terror

5. Possible answers: terrified, huddled, raw and potent, enormous creature, kicked her terror up to another level, incandescent with panic, soupy, heavy, quicksand, like the air in a nightmare

Quick Activity: Primary Source: What If?, p. 148

1. Possible answers: "Education shall forever be encouraged" and "the utmost good faith shall always be observed toward the Indians."

2. The Northwest Ordinance of 1787 prohibits slavery, as well as involuntary servitude.

3. Possible answers: Slavery might have existed in some of the northern part of the country. American Indians might not have been treated well in the northern territories. Education might not have been a priority.

Chapter 8

Quick Activity: Hopi Farming, p. 166

Possible answers:

1. The Hopi developed these methods of farming to make up for the lack of rain in the environment.

2. These methods improve farming in a dry environment by bringing water to areas that need it.

Quick Activity 4: Flags and Mottos, p. 168

Charts should be completed as follows:

State	Flag	Motto
Texas:		*Friendship*
Arizona:		*Ditat Deus* (God enriches)
New Mexico:		*Crescit eundo* (It grows as it goes)
Oklahoma:		*Labor omnia vincit* (Labor conquers all things)

Chapter 9

Quest Activity 1: Yellowstone National Park, p. 182

Possible answers:

rivers: Yellowstone River, Lewis River

lakes: Yellowstone Lake, Shoshone Lake, Lewis Lake, Heart Lake

geysers: Old Faithful, Lone Star Geyser

hot springs: Mammoth Hot Springs

falls: Lewis Falls, Mystic Falls, Kepler Cascades

mountain peaks: Mount Holmes, Mount Norris

Quest Activity 2: Primary Source: Gold Rush, p. 183–184

California: Possible answer: The historic park is interesting because it is the location of the event that caused the West region to grow in the future. People should visit there because they can pan for gold just like miners did long ago.

Klondike: Possible answer: The historic park is interesting because it brings to life the difficulties of the Klondike gold rush. People should visit there because they can hike some of the same trails that gold-seekers walked long ago.

Venn Diagram:

California: clipper ships, people came from eastern cities like New York

Alaska: ships called barks, people departed from eastern cities like New York but could meet the boat at San Francisco or Seattle; cost $680 or more

Both: claimed to be fast, carried people seeking gold

Quest Activity 4: Los Angeles, p. 185

Letter C should be along the Pacific Coast by the Ferris wheel; letter B should be along the coast to the north; letter A should be at the top center of the map; letter D should be the farthest east.

Quick Activity: Alaska's Industries, p. 189

Possible answer: Alaska's economy depends heavily on its natural resources. Its top industries are seafood and oil and gas, all of which are natural resources.

Credits

Image Credits

Chapter 02
040BC: JT Vintage/Glasshouse Images/lamy Stock Photo; 040T: Ian Dagnall/Alamy Stock Photo; 040C: GL Archive/ Alamy Stock Photo; 040B: World History Archive/Alamy Stock Photo; 040TC: George Ostertag/Alamy Stock Photo; 041: Dorothea Lange/Library of Congress Prints and Photographs Division Washington [LC-DIG-ppmsca-12883]

Chapter 04
075: Hera Vintage Ads/Alamy Stock Photo

Chapter 05
099: Everett Collection Historical/Alamy Stock Photo

Chapter 06
116: Afro American Newspapers/Gado/Getty Images; 122: Historical /Corbis Historical/Getty Images

Chapter 07
137: Andriy Kravchenko/Alamy Stock Photo; 138: Andrew Zarivny/Alamy Stock Photo; 139: Jim West/Alamy Stock Photo; 145: Phil Degginger/Alamy Stock Photo; 137: Moreaux.jeje/Panther Media GmbH/Alamy Stock Photo;

138: Moreaux.jeje/Panther Media GmbH/Alamy Stock Photo; 139: Moreaux.jeje/Panther Media GmbH/Alamy Stock Photo

Chapter 08
166T: Hulton Archive/Getty Images; 166B: George H.H. Huey/Alamy Stock Photo; 168TL: Gino's Premium Images/ Alamy Stock Photo; 168TR: Bigalbaloo/YAY Media AS/Alamy Stock Vector; 168BL: Bigalbaloo/YAY Media AS/Alamy Stock Vector; 168BR: Roy Pedersen/Alamy Stock Photo

Text Credits

Woody Guthrie Publications
"This Land Is Your Land" by Woody Guthrie. Words and Music by Woody Guthrie WGP/TRO - © Copyright 1956, 1958, 1970, 1972, and 1995 (copyrights renewed_Woody Guthrie Publications, Inc. & Ludlow Music, Inc., New York, NY. Administered by Ludlow Music, Inc. Used by permission.

Esquire.com
Stories of the Joplin Tornado by Luke Dittrich. Copyright © Esquire.com.